MY WAR

RANDOM HOUSE   NEW YORK

MY WAR

A Love Story in Letters and Drawings

TRACY SUGARMAN

PASSED BY NAVAL CENSOR

U.S. POSTAGE · VIA AIR MAIL · 6¢

All rights reserved under International and Pan American
Copyright Conventions. Published in the United States by
Random House, Inc., New York, and simultaneously in Canada
by Random House of Canada Limited, Toronto.

RANDOM HOUSE and colophon are registered trademarks of
Random House, Inc.

Some of the illustrations in this work were originally published in
Neptunus Rex, published in 1988 by Presidio Press.

Library of Congress Cataloging-in-Publication Data
is available on request.
ISBN 0-375-50513-X

Printed in the United States of America on acid-free paper
Random House website address: www.atrandom.com

9 8 7 6 5 4 3 2

First Edition

FOR JUNE, RICHARD, LAURIE,
CASEY, AMY, AND ABBY

ACKNOWLEDGMENTS

Were it not for a coterie of caring and loving friends, *My War* would never have seen the light of day. More determined midwives do not exist. From 1994, when my sculptor friend Stanley Bleifeld first surveyed my cache of drawings and paintings from World War II, a process was begun that first brought my art and letters to public view. At his urging, the navy was alerted to the work and arranged for a celebratory exhibit at the U. S. Navy Memorial in Washington, D.C., to mark the fiftieth anniversary of D-Day. The intense public interest in the collection was the reason that finally led me to write *My War*.

Finding the rightful home for the book became a committed mission for Bill Buckley, Ellie Buckley, Arthur Singer, Sybil Steinberg, Woody Klein, Alan Neigher, Paul Green, Eleanor Craig, Howard Munce, and, most especially, Jim Schadt. All have been dear friends to our family. I am deeply grateful for their loyalty and dedication.

Shaping the letters and art into a cohesive whole could not have been accomplished without the sensitivity, discretion, and enthusiasm of two remarkably creative people: Marjorie Palmer and Richard Berenson. It has been a wonderful and memorable collaboration.

Finally, I want to acknowledge the love and strength I have received from my son, Richard, my daughter-in-law, Linda, my daughter, Laurie, my son-in-law, David, my amazing granddaughters, Casey, Amy, and Abby, and my dear friend, Gloria Cole. *My War* is for all of them.

PREFACE

I leave it to the historians to chronicle the strategies and dynamics of the global conflict of World War II. With the perspective gained from more than half a century of scholarship, they delineate the battle lines and campaigns, the tactics and struggles of the world I inherited after Pearl Harbor. They know a great deal about "the war." But they didn't live *my* war.

It is my conviction that every sailor and soldier in World War II fought his own war. It was a struggle that only sometimes permitted him to see the enemy. But as he stared out into the darkness from his ship or beachhead, he very soon began to see himself. So new to manhood, he watched himself grow through fear and loneliness, boredom and exaltation. It was an inescapable odyssey for each of us who served.

FOREWORD

THE SCUDDING CLOUDS had shredded in the winter wind, trailing wisps over Long Island Sound. Now the February sun glanced off the water, filling my studio with an unexpected brightness. I leaned back in my chair, squinting at my watercolor, unsure as to what was needed in the new light. I heard June move down the corridor to my studio and stop at the door. She leaned against the doorpost. "You taking a break? Is this a good time to talk?"

I grinned at my wife, still asking after fifty years of my working at home. "Hell, yes. Come on in. I'm drowning in light."

She crossed to my chair and examined the painting on the drawing board. "Looks good," she said. "Still fresh. Don't beat it to death." She pulled up a chair and held up *The New York Times*.

"I just read in the paper that this June will be the fiftieth anniversary of D-Day. Can you believe that?"

I stared at her. "Fiftieth anniversary? No, I can't."

"Well," she smiled, "it must be so. It says so right here in *The New York Times*." She stood up and looked me up and down. "You must be very old. And I must also be very old. *C'est la vie. . . . C'est la guerre.*"

I looked out at the placid expanse of the Sound. At the very edge of the horizon I could see the smudged outline of the Long Island shoreline. "Fifty years since Utah Beach? Jesus!"

June had paused at the door. "It really is. Let's see, we were barely out of college, younger than our granddaughter is right now!"

We both laughed, then I said, "Snoon, what the hell ever happened to the sketchbooks I sent you? All those drawings and watercolor pads?"

"They're in the cellar," she said. "They've been in every cellar of every house we've had. Packed with all your navy letters. The last time we looked at them was when you came home in 1945."

I stared at her. I had no idea she had saved those long-ago sketches. I got up quickly from the board. "You really remember where the D-Day drawings are? I'd like to see them."

June laughed. "Are you that brave? You were very young, honey."

"I'm not that brave. Just curious. Fifty years!"

"Follow me," she said.

The brown paper parcels were right there in the cellar when we went to find them. Patiently waiting inside the wrapping were seventy-seven drawings and watercolors of my part of World War II, along with the letters I'd written to my new bride. Over a span of eighteen months, those fragile bits of paper had crossed the Atlantic Ocean while packs of German U-boats were ravaging the Allied shipping lanes. Upon receiving them, June would scan the drawings and letters avidly, seeking clues as to where I was and how I was.

For fifty years, the art and the four hundred letters had been out of sight and out of mind. I knew that the hundreds of letters June had sent me during the war had never made it back. Like most servicemen and women, I simply had no place to store the precious pieces from home.

But June had managed to save everything I sent her. And when I tore open the brittle wrappings in 1994, I found my own Baedeker to a time when June and I were both twenty-one, and the war was the only world we knew.

MY WAR

EVERYBODY REMEMBERS exactly where they were that Sunday. You sensed immediately that there had been a subtle shift in the world, a movement you could almost feel in your bones. What it would portend would come later. For that split second, the whole room simply froze. It's funny what you remember. Davey Beere, his face beet red from running across the campus, tore into our fraternity house. "They bombed Pearl Harbor!" he gasped. And somebody said, "Who the hell is Pearl Harbor?"

Davey dropped onto a leather couch and shook his head vehemently. "Not who. What, idiot. Pearl Harbor is our navy base in Hawaii." His eyes widened. "And the radio says it's the Japs that did it."

"How bad is it?" I asked.

"They didn't say," said Davey. "They just said this means we're in the war." The room was dead silent. "In the war," said Davey.

Two days later I boarded the early morning train to Buffalo, found my way to the navy office, and took the physical exam for the naval reserve. It was the middle of my junior year at Syracuse University. I was studying to be an illustrator in the College of Fine Arts, and I was learning so much. How to draw, how to paint, how to see! And now, suddenly, the leisurely cadence of college life gave way to an unfamiliar urgency. My graduation seemed very far in the distance, so far that I wondered if I would ever get there.

And here I was, signing up to be a naval officer, a guy who had never even seen a ship up close!

The chief petty officer, hashmarks on his unbuttoned blouse, listlessly studied my application after I passed the physical. He nodded to the chair by his desk, and I sat down. In a distracted voice he asked, "Can you believe those Japs? Hitting Pearl? That was my base for seventeen months! My base! And all those guys . . ." He stopped abruptly. The room was silent as he turned back to my transcript. "What the hell are you doing at college?" he asked curtly. "And what is fine arts? Like drafting, for engineers?"

I didn't know what to say. "No," I muttered finally, "it's more like . . . camouflage. Stuff like that." I got up quickly. "Gotta catch my train back to Syracuse." I held out my hand. "Thanks, sir."

The CPO rose and leaned heavily against his desk. "No. No," he said. "Not sir. I ain't a commissioned officer. I'm a noncommissioned officer. Commissioned officers is sir. You understand? *Commissioned officers.*" He watched my face and then said kindly, "You just call me Chief."

"Right," I said. "Thank you, Chief," and tossed him a salute.

He stared at me. "No," he groaned. "No. No. No. You don't

salute noncommissioned officers. You salute commissioned officers." He sat down heavily and stared at the stack of papers waiting to be processed. "Commissioned officers," he growled, "like *you're* going to be." As he reached for the pile, I ducked out the door.

THREE WEEKS after I had joined the naval reserve, I took June Feldman for a ride in my old man's De Soto. June was a slender, smart, tawny blond classmate, with hazel eyes. She had the quiet assurance of a young woman who has always been beautiful, but you sensed very quickly that her beauty was of no real consequence to her. There was something about her, a certain gravity that separated her from the pretty butterflies alighting on campus, and when you were admitted to her friendship, you felt privileged.

In the first weeks of our freshman year, June became the girlfriend of my best friend, Shelly, and I was glad for both of them.

June and Shelly were the couple I double-dated with most until the first months of our junior year. She and I became dear friends, and she often served as my social guide, offering well-researched data about the coeds I should date. Before Christmas vacation of that year, Shelly gave her his fraternity pin, an act in 1941 that practically meant an engagement. June, being June, searched her heart over the holiday and acted on what she found. With characteristic honesty, she informed my best friend on her return back to campus that she did not truly love him and gave him back his pin. This social drama was being played out at the very time I was in Buffalo, joining the U.S. Naval Reserve.

June
on a snowy day,
Syracuse University, 1942

5

When I got back to the university and my fraternity house, I found that June had been totally ostracized by Shelly's large circle of friends. "Nobody talks to Feldman," was the word. I thought this banishment was cruel and unusual punishment, and I broke ranks with my brothers. I called her and assured her that I was still her friend, and that I'd be by in half an hour to pick her up.

"Are you sure you know what you're doing, Sug?" she asked.

I said I was certain I didn't, but I could borrow my old man's De Soto and we could talk about it. I drove her out to the lakes beyond town, to a tiny bar in Cazenovia, where we began a conversation that was to last a lifetime.

It was the first of our explorations of the villages and rolling countryside of upstate New York. The old De Soto was roomy, gas was fifteen cents a gallon, and soon we became a couple who were very much in love. Friend Shelly was involved with a new girlfriend and slowly the exiling of June began to diminish. Before long we reentered the circle of old comrades.

There are so many golden images that float behind my eyes when I remember those last years on campus. They're fragrant with burning autumn leaves and the delicious smell of new grass after the endless Syracuse winter snow finally melted away. And when the memories come, often unsummoned, I see June again, in saddle shoes and cashmere sweaters, and we're listening to Tommy Dorsey or dancing to Glenn Miller as he plays our song, "Moonlight Cocktail."

Ours was the generation of the big bands—Goodman, the Dorsey brothers, Claude Thornhill, Count Basie, Hal Kemp. We memorized the lyrics on the Hit Parade, bought the clunky seventy-eights, and played them until they were gray and scratchy. And we danced—in dorm living rooms, at proms, in fraternity houses and sorority houses. We were so grateful to the Hoagy Carmichaels, Harold Arlens, Lorenz Harts, who said romantically what we longed to say, and to the great bands that swept us tight together, arms about each other, onto a dance floor, exactly where we wanted to be.

How very young and innocent most of us were. Dancing, body to body, cheek to cheek, to "In the Mood" or "Sentimental Journey" was as close to real sexual gratification as most of us were likely to get. It would be decades before the Pill would redefine acceptable behavior. For those of us in the 1940s who were in love, romance and fantasy were the best we could manage. And while dancing helped, it was still hell having to wait until we could "make it legal."

Time floated past as the two of us enjoyed the drama of the changing seasons, said good-bye to buddies who were being called up by the army, the marines, the air force, and jealously collected the hours we could spend together. We talked endlessly, about race, music, religion, politics, my painting, her hopes for a career in South America, and always "When will the navy cut all this short?" Incredibly, the days stretched into a year, and then all the way to graduation.

On May 11, 1943, fittingly in a Syracuse snow shower, we graduated together. And on May 13, I reported to midshipman school at Notre Dame University in Indiana. The work was tough, but the comradeship was great. I was quickly dubbed "McSugarman"—to fit in with all the McCarthys and McMahons. Wouldn't my Jewish fraternity brothers get a kick out of that?

Indiana was the farthest from home I had ever traveled, and the

distance from June was excruciating. Not surprisingly, by July we decided to get married and at least have some time together before I went to war. We broke the news to our startled parents, certain that we knew best. On September 22, I received my commission as an Ensign, USNR. Two days later, we were married in front of still startled parents and friends, had a one-day honeymoon at the Biltmore Hotel—no curfew, no housemother—and took a train to Solomon Island, Maryland, my first navy base.

FOR THE NEXT FOUR MONTHS, we led the frantic, marginal life of young service couples caught up in the war. Overseas departure was always imminent, and hours together were cherished and rare.

My days were spent on the frigid waters of the Chesapeake Bay, training sailors for the upcoming invasion of Europe. Our boats were "small boats," LCVPs (landing craft, vehicle, personnel), a long name for a very simple craft. Thirty-six feet in length and eleven feet wide, they were designed to carry either a single vehicle or thirty soldiers onto a beach. They were open to every breaking wave and drop of sleet-filled rain, but we learned to handle the awkward craft in every conceivable kind of weather and light. LCVPs were built out of plywood, with a draft of only three feet. The deck had a sheathing of metal, and the square bow door was made of steel. Racing toward an enemy beachhead, that steel door would be our only shield. Once we hit the beach, it would be lowered to serve as a ramp for the cargo we carried. Like all amphibious vessels in the war, the LCVPs were able to ride onto a beach and to pull themselves off.

Our boats had two circular turrets flanking the bow door, designed to hold .30-caliber machine guns. Early in our training,

Opposite:
A toast to the bride,
September 24, 1943

however, we found that in such shallow-draft boats there was no possible way to fire the guns accurately. Our mission was not to engage the enemy. It was to keep these vital craft afloat so they could perform the thousand tasks that would be needed once hostilities began. It was tough and arduous work, but it gave us what we would need when the great moment came overseas.

While my sailors and I were churning up the waters of the Chesapeake, June and several of the officers' wives volunteered to man the air detection center in Norfolk. American ships were constantly being sunk by German submarines just off the coast, so the threat of other possible enemy attacks seemed very real. Monitoring the air traffic in the area was important work, but the days for most of the women were long and tedious. When I'd return from the Bay to our room in Ocean View, Virginia, June would be back from her day, eager to see her new husband. I was just as anxious to hold my new bride, but I was also exhausted and chilled from the boats. I'd struggle to keep awake in the overheated apartment, but too often it was a losing battle. Much too soon, June would wake me so I could make the five-thirty bus back to base at Little Creek.

On one memorable occasion, I finished a night exercise out on the Bay at ten o'clock, caught a ten-thirty bus back to Ocean View, and surprised my delighted partner when I walked in at eleven fifteen. We made wonderful love, set the clock for five twenty a.m., and fell deep asleep. When the alarm went off, I grabbed my clothes, kissed my sleeping wife good-bye, and bolted for the bus. When I arrived at the base in Little Creek, I noticed that the whole camp was asleep. I stopped to sign in with the shore patrolman at the gate.

"Where's everybody, sailor? The whole place looks dead."

"Sir?" he said. "Dead? No, sir. It always looks like that at one-thirty in the morning."

One-thirty? One-thirty! I'd been home for less than an hour and a half when that damn alarm clock went off!

"You all right, sir?" asked the shore patrolman.

"Yeah. Sure. Just a little sleepy. Good night." And I headed for the silent barracks.

LATE IN JANUARY 1944, orders came directing our whole outfit to move out. We had all trained exhaustively and were eager to get to the English staging areas. The invasion could not be far away. As we were packing to leave the base, unsettling new orders arrived. Two other ensigns, Tommy Wolfe and "Andy" Anderson, and I were detached from the group and ordered to await a new bunch of sailors who would be coming for amphibious training. It was a compliment to our skill as officers, but disappointing because we had honed our crews over months of hard work, and now they were leaving without us. The good news was that perhaps my time with June would be extended for weeks, or even months. It was with mixed feelings that we watched our gang board a long convoy of trucks, wave good-bye, and head for a troopship in Norfolk.

Only three days later, additional orders arrived that threw us completely. Three officers and thirty men were to "proceed immediately to Long Beach, New York, to await transport to the European Theater of Operations." Tommy, Andy, and I were bewildered. All the crews had already gone. The only enlisted men still at Little Creek were in the navy brig or were awaiting trials in summary court or general court martial. In the strange workings of navy bureaucracy, thirty of those prisoners were released to our charge. We were to train them and take them to war. Thirty men were needed, and thirty men they got. Orders were orders!

WE WERE NEVER SHOWN the personal dossiers of the new men, but the anecdotal histories soon became common scuttlebutt. Some of it was hair-raising. Stories of armed robbery, criminal violence, even rape, were passed with the coffee at chow. I listened to the stories, studied their faces, and tried in vain to determine what was true and what was youthful bravado. I finally took my buddy and fellow ensign, Tommy Wolfe, aside.

A tough, street-smart New York kid himself, Tommy looked and sounded like Jimmy Cagney. He grinned at my concern about our new crews. "Relax, Sug. This is the biggest break these characters could dream of. If we're tough and fair with them, they'll work out great. I grew up with guys like them."

The problem I had was that growing up in Syracuse, I had never really known guys from the streets. I had lived a kind of Norman Rockwell adolescence, buffered from scenarios where violence was the way of survival. The only violence I was familiar with was the physical contact on a university lacrosse field. At the end of a tough game, you shook hands; you didn't protect your back. I was a hard-nosed defense man, and I had learned I could give as well as take. But I wondered how, at twenty-two, I could make these men believe I was tough enough to take them to war.

On the train north to New York, June rode with the released prisoners. At the first opportunity, I took her aside. "Are you okay? They giving you a hard time?"

She laughed. "They're kids," she said. "They're tough kids. I wouldn't want to be the Germans when they hit the beach. But they're really very sweet."

I stared at my wife. "Sweet?"

"Well," she said, grinning, "they're very sweet to me."

OUR FEW DAYS TOGETHER in Long Beach were bittersweet. June and I were greedy for our hours together, but we knew that our time was running out. The night before I had to leave, she watched me pack my seabag in silence and then, smiling, handed me a brown paper package. "Put this on the top," she said. "It's a little something for both of us."

I edged open the package and peered inside. Sketch pads! And pens and a tin of watercolors!

"How wonderful! You're too much, Junie. But those are for me. What's for you?"

June tilted her head and embraced me. Very quietly she said, "For me it's your sanity. And maybe some pictures so that I'll know you're alive and kicking! Hold on real tight, darling. You'll be back and I'll be waiting."

Before the dawn, I hoisted my seabag, kissed my new wife good-bye, and left for the troop train. June found an apartment in Greenwich Village, got a job at Chemical Bank, and settled in for the long hard months ahead.

A summer day at Ocean View

EN ROUTE
TO WAR

THE QUEEN MARY

O UR BLACKED-OUT TROOP TRAIN chugged through a chill February night to a darkened siding near the Hudson River. For days, rumor had it that we were going to England aboard the *Queen Mary*, the fastest ship in the world in 1944. But we never knew for sure until the train was under way. My tough little cadre of felons and I were only one group among 14,000 troops slated to board the *Queen Mary*. The ship would go without a convoy because of her capacity to outrun the wolf packs of German submarines which were devastating our shipping lanes. Before debarking the train, I scribbled my first letter to June.

En route to the Queen Mary

We're almost to our ship. Train ride rather unexciting—kids expectant but quiet. We've gotten a break: found out that the ship we're getting is the one we had heard all the scuttlebutt about. Be where we're going quick as the dickens! Nothing seems to be adequate. I think I'll say nothing more, my sweetheart. Just thank you—and God bless you. Beginning to breathe the adventure of this business. I'm glad. Whatever I see, I'll write to you if possible. The rest I'll save up to share with you. Must close, darling. Almost in. Take everything in stride, Junie.

LIFE ABOARD the *Queen Mary* was surreal. Fourteen thousand men and women were jammed into every crevice and corner of a rolling, reeking, stripped-down grand hotel. At night, portholes were blacked out as the ship, motors throbbing, rocked across a very rough North Atlantic. The ship's great staircases were thronged with soldiers, sailors, nurses, WAACs, journalists; and the once-elegant salons were bedlam. Many of the passengers were violently seasick, suddenly polluting a packed area of humanity. Traveling alone and unprotected, the *Mary* would alter course at frequent intervals, tilting the whole landscape and perspective as the vessel drove through the mounting seas. We would clutch handrails, eyes closed, waiting for the ship to right itself.

In the areas reserved for the navy and army officers, the packing of humanity was somewhat more manageable. Four of us junior officers shared a stateroom designed for two. In a tiny alcove of the cabin was a tiny bathtub. After I had been pitched from my upper-deck bunk by the heaving of the ship, I appropriated the little tub as my bunk. There was room, however, in the dining area for a bridge game that went on continuously. And there was a poker game, played on our bunks, where I learned that poker was a game I had no right playing. In the maelstrom of the enlisted men's quarters, one of my best and brightest from the Norfolk brig set himself up as the House, and ran a nonstop crap game on his blanket. Before we left the *Mary*,

Opposite:
Poker game aboard the Queen Mary

This page:
An army bunk
mate

Opposite:
Army and navy
in the Officers'
Lounge
aboard ship

20

Above and opposite:
At life jacket drill

he came to me seeking some protection for his new-won wealth, twenty-seven hundred dollars. At the first opportunity, I wired the money home to his mother.

When possible during the stormy days, we would scramble outside to the promenade deck, trading the frigid soaking of the February storm for the chance to breathe fresh, salty air. The seas were mammoth, more formidable than any movie had prepared me for. Our great powerful vessel, belching smoke from her huge stacks, felt tiny in the racing swells. We'd search the gray-green mountains of water and wonder if somewhere under there a German sub was launching a torpedo. Nervously we'd recheck our flimsy life jackets and finally hurry back inside to the noise, the shouting, the laughter, and the warmth of the human cargo. For my first trip outside of the U.S.A., I had lots of company.

On the Way—Aboard the Queen Mary

I'm sharing the general air of holiday spirit that's prevalent aboard—casual, unconcerned, remote. You have to pinch yourself to realize that you are actually going overseas, that you are actually in danger of attack—that all these guys who you are sleeping, eating, playing poker with are actually going to war! There is just a great deal of laughing—total lack of tension or hysteria.

The ocean is tremendous—about the most trite way of saying the obvious! But that's all you can say. It's tremendous and powerful. So powerful it makes our ship minute in its insignificance. If there were a thousand ships like this, or ten thousand, they would still be a ridiculous man-made impudence on all this gorgeous, churning immensity. It makes you philosophical, darling, and quite aware of the very Lilliputian qualities of man and man-made things. The only thing that isn't insignificant about Lilliputian man is what he thinks, what he feels, what he wants, whether he can achieve it or not. That he dreams, that he experiences—these are the important things. They give him the majesty not found in his cities or in his monuments. His ideas, his dreams leap this tremendous sea and are as unconcerned with its boilings and its swells and its roar as is truth undisturbed by distortions and camouflage. Truth and man's beauty alone transcend the naked beauty of primitive nature. If I were to drown right this minute, it would be no great loss. It would be only one more man-animal engulfed in the ferocity of nature. But what I dreamed of seeing, of doing, what I had to create which was never created, what I might have given—these are the things that would make it tragic, that make it important I don't get lost.

Whoosh! How wordy. Forgive me, Junie.

Sometime in February—Aboard the Queen Mary
Tomorrow we arrive—a new and exciting period, something completely new. New people, customs, habits. I'm looking forward to it expectantly, eagerly. I want to see all I can. I've done quite a lot of sketching on the Mary. I want to do more if I can make the time. Don't fret, sweetheart. Things so far could not be better.

We landed in Scotland and immediately boarded a train for England. The only Scot we saw was a cute red-cheeked lass who was passing out coffee for the Red Cross. What we saw of Scotland from the train windows was very beautiful, perfectly ordered and laid out. Darkness came early and we rode until ten the next morning.

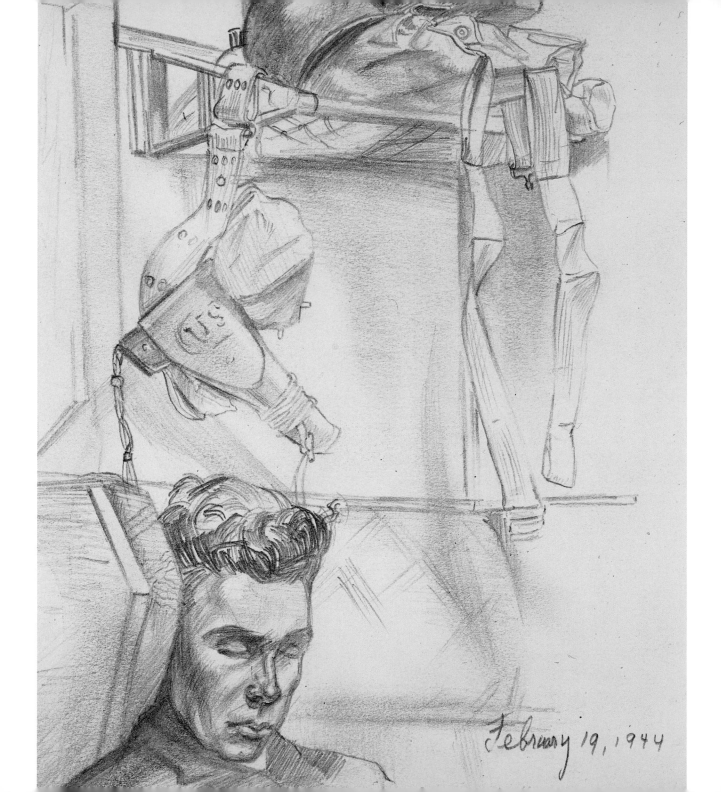

February 19, 1944

February 20—En route to Plymouth, England

How are you, my wonderful Snoon? Lemme tell you wots been 'appening to yer ever lovin' spouse—tell yer, that is, within the limits of military security. I'm not where we guessed I'd be. I'm in England! And England has pleased me so far.

I got on a drawing jag that carried over onto the train and is still keeping my fingers itchy. Was wonderful, and the sketchbook is damn near loaded already! The whole trip has been a series of impressions that should be invaluable later. Baby, I've found out I can draw again, and watch our dust when I come back!

The train ride was delightful. Saw some of the most magnificent countryside I'd ever imagined. The most vivid impression overall is orderly loveliness, villages of stone houses, each with its vegetable garden and stone wall; narrow, winding, wall-lined roads; white stucco farm buildings; scrubbed stoops; hardly a tree out of place. Each bit of the countryside lovingly and tenderly plotted out. We would pass vistas of rolling hills, every shade of green spotted with furrowed acres of rich sienna brown, black-and-umber patches of woods, squares of green forest preserves, and the whole landscape crossed and patterned with long, low stone walls that raced the train. How completely entranced we all were. It was different somehow—quaint, quiet, unpretentious. You felt it had always been so. It is no wonder to me that the Englishman loves his England. It is beautiful.

Left: Forty winks on a troop train

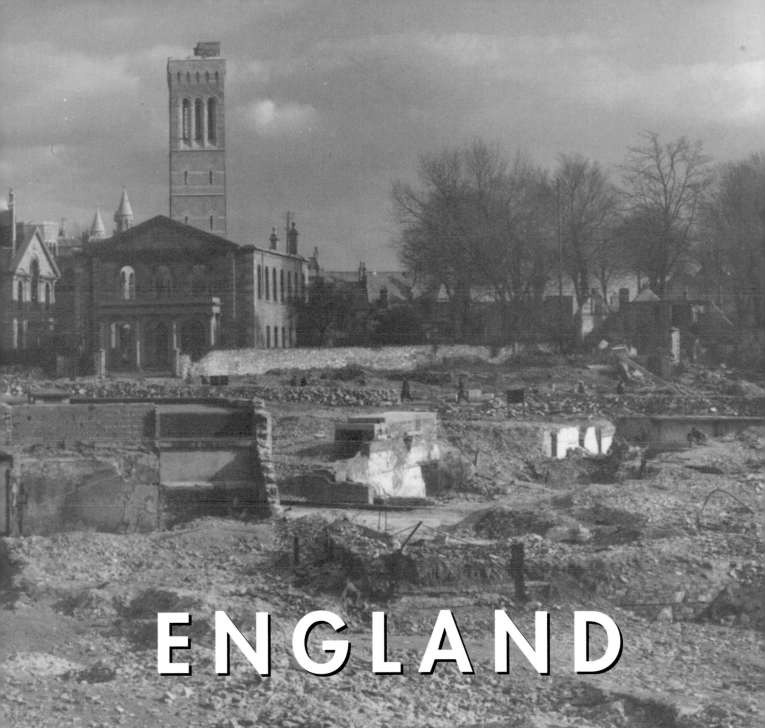

ENGLAND

WAITING FOR D-DAY

IT WAS A SUNDAY when we arrived in Plymouth. The city had caught hell in the blitz, and the men and I looked around doubtfully at the wrecked and gutted ruins that used to be homes and schools and churches. Our first question was "When did you have your last raid?" They told us last November, so we breathed easier. We climbed into trucks and went to the base, a motley assortment of Quonset huts on the top of a hill on the outskirts of town. Below us was a river, and across the river was a little old town where I would later find plenty that caught my eye. The view was glorious. Rolling hills as far as the eye could see.

February 21—Plymouth

Had a wonderful time today, darling. Tommy and I took a sightseeing tour of the nearest town. The people we've met here have been very nice. They've had a long, tough war, and they look considerably

Opposite:
Street scene in Plymouth

dowdier than our people back home. Clothes are rationed, and they're mended and put on again. Two ounces of butter per week per person. All of us feel slightly ashamed of our total divorce from real sacrifice. I told a girl in the canteen of our 1/2 lb. of butter per person per week and her eyes opened like saucers. I don't believe they resent that sort of thing. It's merely inconceivable to them. Next time I think I'll hesitate to speak of conditions at home unless I'm asked.

29

I'm cutting my way through a maze of pounds, thruppence, shillings, ha'pennies, pennies, florins—ad infinitum, ad exhaustion! There's a terrible temptation to treat the paper money like the stuff you use in a Monopoly game. It doesn't look real. But it bought a good lamb dinner at the hotel for about a crown—a dollar in our money. When we have to pay the check, we take out our bankroll, extend it and say, "Take what I owe you."

The illusion of still being home persists—and it's really only at night during the blackouts that you realize you are in England. You literally can't see your hand in front of your face, and you walk into walls and people. Leave it to the American sailors to utilize every dark moment! The women are many, and liberty is closest in spirit to "call of the wild." Me? Well, just guess, partner. What do you think?

February 22—Plymouth

I can't seem to drink in enough local color. How I wish I could record it all! The pink-kneed, pink-cheeked kids, smaller than kids at home, with lots of hair—mostly blond, it seems. Too many with pinched faces. They swarm around. "Penny, mister? Got some gum?" The minute you reach in your pocket—who can say no to kids—they multiply like rabbits and you find yourself leading a caravan of Oliver Twists down the street.

Then there's the magic of young people in the blackouts, just the fleeting glimpse of hurrying couples, very close, framed in the light of a passing army truck. The old emptiness of English streets at night, the crowded push of men in uniform crammed into the back of a blacked-out lorry, racing through a dark countryside, just the wisplike flicker of light rolling across their backs, their cheeks. An eye

This page and opposite:
Plymouth in wartime

31

that catches the light and seems to hold it in its pupil for a moment, and then it's gone and you're rattling along through the night again. Then there is the uniformity of neighborhoods, each house quite content to rub shoulders with houses which look exactly as she does. And they repeat and repeat until you have an elephant-like uniformity that circles a hill and climbs over and beyond the crest. But in their uniformity is an order and a unity that is somehow extremely English to me. Each house supports the next, and yet when you glance inside they are completely personal, warm—comfortable. The English seem like that—quite alike, rather drab; but when you talk to one, you are surprised by the warmth of his smile. It's always surprising. And it's nice.

February 24—Plymouth

After chow, I took my sketch pad and went hunting. Three sketches and three promising results! You remember how I used to get in the groove sometimes, and no matter what I was doing, it just had to turn out right? Well since I left the States, it's been that way and I'm praying the charm sticks for a while. I did 2 ragamuffin girls, age 7— Iris Rose Mary Oskin and Sandra Bond—at the expense of one penny to Oskin and a halfpenny to Sandra. I had run out of pennies. The demand is terrific. When they asked me, "What are you takin' our picture for, Yank?" I told them that I wanted to show my wife, way over in America, what pretty little girls they have in England. This pleased them and they posed as graciously as the Queen herself.

Opposite: Sandra (left) and Iris Rose Mary

Overleaf: Barrage balloons over Plymouth

JUNE'S FAREWELL GIFT of art materials turned out to be a comforting connection to who I was and what I had left behind. Whenever I could steal the time on liberties or leave, all that surrounded me, however banal, became grist for my mill. The kids, the villages, the barrage balloons, the pubs, and doughnut wagons, all went into the sketchbooks and got sent home to June. How bizarre to recall those first liberties in Plymouth as I shuffled through the rubble of bombed-out neighborhoods, making drawings. And wandered into the pubs where I'd trade speculations with the resolute Englishmen about the coming "second front," or if the Russians could hold off the German panzer divisions that had overrun the whole European continent. In every direction, the mass of matériel from America was growing, burying the meadows with trucks and tanks and ammunition. The recurrent joke in our Quonset huts was: "When they cut the cables of all these barrage balloons, this whole damn island is going to sink!"

March 1—Plymouth

Dozed off after dinner tonight, only to be wakened by the strains of "Daddy, you oughta get the best for me!" It was a doughnut wagon run by the Red Cross that visits camps with fresh doughnuts and coffee, and corny old music. Made a quick sketch, had 2 cups of java and 6 doughnuts. Later, I stepped out of our Quonset hut and drank in the cool air. I let the beauty of the night soak over me. It was a liquid dark night. Clouds scudded across the moon, and stars clustered around the edges and gazed, wide-eyed, down. I wandered away from the camp. Nowhere to be seen were the lighted windows of stateside. Instead, the moon laid her cold light hand on a roof, a

Above: Lining up for fresh doughnuts and old music
Opposite: One of the navy's finest

wall, a field, rolled over and beyond the sleeping pond. And where she had been was a pool of liquid dark, a play of darks that made the lights of the white moon ever more white.

Sometime in March—Plymouth
Tonight I broke out the water-colors for the first time. A scene from downtown. Played with the dusk and the funny effects of flashlights on a darkening city. What I want to get here is just impressions with color—ideas... fast, simple.

Dusk in the city, 1944

"Home"

march 6, 1944

The Greenbank Hotel.

EARLY IN MARCH, orders came to proceed from the hills beyond Plymouth to the village of Fowey in Cornwall. It was time to get our crews back into boats again, and to start the maneuvers that would simulate the D-Day invasion, which now felt imminent.

Fowey was a beautiful spot, built on incredibly steep hills around the harbor. In town, the streets were just wide enough for our jeeps to pass. It was very old, very quaint, and very dull. There was only one movie house, where you had to have reservations, and a couple of tea shops with horrible wartime pastries.

The Greenbank Hotel,
my home in Fowey

Above:
USO entertainer

Opposite:
View from my window

March 6—Fowey, England

Am settled in front of our lovely fireplace in a room in an old summer hotel. A swell setup, 2 double-decker bunks in the room, tall windows overlooking the little harbor down below. The barny feeling is offset by 2 soft chairs and our own fireplace! No central heating, no private johns, but quaint as an 1890 beer garden! I got the big sunny room in the front by insisting on cutting cards. I drew a king, Tommy a queen, Lars a 9, Andy a 4, and Frank a deuce. Heh! Heh! I am now ensconced in comparative luxury.

March 9—Fowey

The quaintness of the towns here is almost touched by magic at night. Narrow alleyways, sharp deep shadows, angles, and rooftops and chimney pots—the blackouts send them back to their medieval aura, like something you dreamed once. I hope so long as I am here to see it, England keeps its oldness, its strangeness.

Yesterday morning Tommy and I went downtown and in our wanderings came across the most beautiful daffodils. We bought a dozen and brought them back to the room. I searched high and low for something to put them in and couldn't find a thing. So I filled one of our trench helmets half full of water, and now the daffodils are reposing beautifully in their new home! Would make quite a still life!

March 10—Fowey

Just got back from a real funny USO camp show and had a wonderful time. Three gals, strictly from Coney Island and Brooklyn; a very funny comedian, Willy Shore; and some solid trumpetin' and

43

stompin'! I do miss you, Snoon, so very much, but it's things like the show tonight that snap a guy out of himself.

It is so hard for me to give you a real three-dimensional look at what it's like to be living overseas. Somehow when I was in the States, "overseas" was a word, and it was an emotional sort of connotation for me. Stuff like "give a prayer for the guys over there" or "in Flanders fields where poppies grow" would somehow sneak into my mind. It was impossible to visualize the actuality, the realness, of living 24 hours a day "overseas." I thought "being overseas" was a series of emotional rides, kind of a newsreel kaleidoscope—never quite real, never lasting longer than a moment. But life here is stepping into the sunshine or drizzles or cold wind, going to chow, lighting a Chesterfield with my coffee. It's looking around at hills, at guys, at automobiles. It's laboring trucks shifting gears and somebody near you saying, "Son of a bitch, I'm sleepy." It's realizing that America is "overseas" to these people. Can you understand what I am saying, Junie? I'm not slogging through mud or marching to bands or leaning out of train windows and waving. I'm just living.

March 19—Fowey
Time is going surprisingly fast for me. All of a sudden every week it's Sunday, and I can't remember what happened to the rest of the days. Have been keeping at the sketch pad and that eats away the time. Did a drawing of Tommy doing his laundry. Out to sea this afternoon for maneuvers. It was so beautiful, and tonight I sport the first stages of an honest-to-God sunburn!

Opposite:
Tommy and his laundry,
with daffodils

44

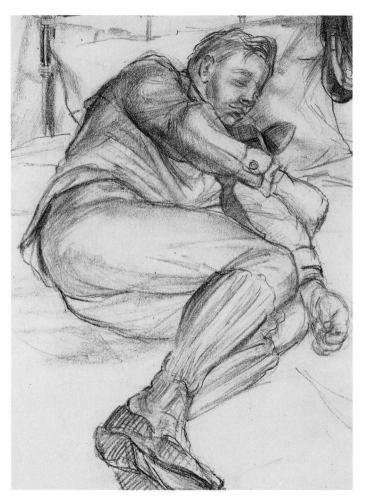

Sack duty

March 21—Fowey

A hectic week of work on the boats. The result as far as your husband is concerned, Mrs. Sugarman, is an enormous appetite and a delicious yen to sleep! I'm pooped. It's a real break from the waiting around routine of the past few months, and it feels wonderful to be active again. Got complimented for my job today and I was very pleased. Tonight every muscle is just as weary as hell, but inside I feel warm and my whole body is filled with a feeling of well-being.

March 28—Fowey

Went over to the rec hut for the USO show on the base here tonight, and they announced that it was USO policy to seat all the enlisted men first. There wasn't room for everyone, so I left. It's as it should be. My kids get few enough privileges, and we certainly have no reason to bitch.

Today was a lovely shiny day, and I had more fun in the boats than I've had in months! The sea was running pretty high, and I took a turn at the wheel myself for a change. Cracked the waves wide open, drenched myself and had a glorious time! Nothing quite like it to make your blood race and build your appetite, man!

March 29—Fowey

Going crazy waiting, hon. The kids here in the hut who haven't been home in about a year and a half have launched a campaign of "simulated war neurosis" in order to get home. In the middle of chow or a crap game or a muster, one of them will suddenly look up real startled and say, "What are bugles blowing for? Listen. Shhh!" Or "Did you bring those butterflies in here?" Everything stops and all the guys fall in with the gag. I'll guarantee that the whole base will be nuts in a week!

April 6—Fowey

Starting at 3:30 this coming morn, I'm getting up to go to sea again! Yep, we're going to start working for a living again. Maneuvers are usually fun, though. If I can only find my way down to the docks at that horrible hour through this bloomin' Limey blackout, I'll be okay.

When I got off watch last night, I came back up to the hut and reread five of your letters, darling. I've been doing that almost every night for the past week, and they make up the loveliest part of the day for me. I'm warmed and excited by the almost tangible presence of you in each one. I fall asleep wrapped in that loveliness.

April 14—Fowey

These madmen I live with have been on a revival singing binge, a sequel to the "bugles" and "butterflies." The hut rocks at all hours with "Old Time Religion," "Brighten the Corner Where You Are," "Beulah Land—Sweet Beulah Land," and "The Old Rugged Cross." In desperation I'm becoming a Baptist or a Methodist—don't know which—but the singing goes on and on, even during the crap games!

Above: Our laundry boy
Overleaf: The jetty in Fowey

47

"The Jetty"

Above:
Ensign "Andy" Anderson

Opposite:
LCVPs practicing on the
Fowey beachhead

F OR FOUR WEEKS the work was intensive with our boats at Fowey. Moving out into the often angry chop of the English Channel, our LCVPs would circle endlessly off an English beachhead before getting the green light from a guide boat, which would send us crashing through the waves in a simulated assault. After hitting the beach, we'd struggle to pull ourselves back to the breaking waves, reassemble out in the Channel, and do it again. And again. The repetition of maneuvers was exhausting, so we were more than happy when we finally got orders to report aboard ship, the ship that would be our home until D-Day.

Ever since our arrival we had observed the steady buildup of ships and boats in every little port along the Devon and Cornwall coast. For any new ship coming into the traffic around Dartmouth, Weymouth, Plymouth, Fowey, or Salcombe, it took real skill and seamanship to even find a space to tie up overnight. Of all the towns, my great favorite was Salcombe. It was small, quaint, very beautiful, and the countryside around it was dazzling. It would be our home base until we sailed off with the great armada on D-Day.

And what an armada it was, assembled out of a desperate ingenuity. When America entered World War II in December 1941, the Japanese commanded the Pacific, and the Nazis had overrun all of Europe except Russia and England. Denied port facilities in both theaters of operations—ports which would be vital for any invasion of Europe and Japan—the Allies had to find means to facilitate a successful assault. Winston Churchill conceived the need for amphibious craft which could do that job. But it was American ingenuity that created an impressive series of vessels that could carry massive numbers of men and matériel onto enemy beaches, transforming them

"The Beach"
April 3rd.

51

into makeshift ports and marshaling yards.

The largest of these ships were the LSTs (landing ship, tank), long, gray, awkward vessels. They were almost ten yards longer than a football field, and fifty feet in width. Our small invasion craft, the LCVPs, were carried on davits on each side of the vessel. Manned by four sailors in each, the boats would be lowered to the water, where they would attempt to hover close by the mother ship (the LST). Their job was to assist the soldiers scrambling down the cargo nets into the boats and then carry the men safely to their destination.

The LSTs' main function was to carry tanks, trucks, jeeps, half-tracks, food, ammunition, hospitals, and troops onto the enemy beachhead once it was secured. Day after day after day, the great unlovely ships would drive onto the beach. The great bow doors would swing out, and out would pour all the tools of war that would keep the invasion inland fed, armed, and moving ahead. Without the LSTs, the invasion of Europe and the conquest of the Japanese would have been impossible.

Opposite:
Offloading an LST

April 16—Fowey

Big news at last! I'm leaving the base and going aboard ship, LST 491, finally! My land-based sailoring of the past nine months is now drawing to a close. And good riddance, I say! It's been dull and repetitious, and the men get bored and sloppy. A case of rigor mortis sets in that isn't healthy. Tom and I will be on adjacent ships. Unluckily, we won't be shipping together as planned. We both feel badly about it, but there's nothing that can be done. At least we'll be in the same flotilla.

I'm excited about the change—new faces, new problems, new experiences. I want to expose myself over and over again to new things. The time it takes to see, absorb, and file takes up the slack of "missing" somewhat, and I hope we move around a lot. The 491 will be my home for a long while, I suspect.

Met a chap by the name of Dwight Sheppler last night at the base. He's one of a very few official naval war painters and has been through action in the Pacific and Med. I couldn't help but envy his job, the most marvelous break an artist could hope to get. My work is of necessity sketchy on-the-spot stuff. To have the opportunity for developing finished work is really some break. This morning at his request I brought some of my sketches over for him to see. I was kind of leery of showing them. It's been so long since anyone but the Philistines have seen my work. Happily, his evaluation of those sketches he thought had merit coincided with my own, so maybe I'm still uncorrupted.

I'm looking forward to shipboard life. I should have both the opportunity and the time to myself to do some drawing and painting. I hope so.

April 18—LST 491

Well, angel, it's finally happened. I'm actually aboard a naval vessel at last. I can't tell you what a wonderful feeling it is. I'm part of more than a Boy Scout camp in Little Creek. The officers are an interesting and unusually mature bunch. They should wear well, I think. My fellow small-boat officer, a chap called Danny Buttabaugh (they call him Badger) is a most considerate guy, really going out of his way to get me established. The skipper is a short, dynamic guy who seems to

The Captain, LST 491

know exactly what he wants. My duties will be primarily concerned with my men and their boats, but I'll stand regular watches and should have the opportunity to use some of the things I sweated out in midshipman school.

Being part of an active and living organism should help push away the blues that sneak up when you're doing nothing. My men are like different guys already. It's incredible how much difference there is in a sailor on land and the same kid aboard ship. They feel after all those months of waiting that they're finally being given a chance to be sailors, and they love it. The ship is magnificently equipped and the boats are damn near perfect. I share a cabin with Badger. There are about 10 officers aboard, plus a doctor. I'll keep you posted on my reactions to the "brothers in arms."

April 19—LST 491

I broke out my sketch pads tonight. Hope to start work on some drawings tomorrow. Now that I'm finally settled, I'm going to send the filled sketch books home to you so you can share a little of what I've seen. The censor says it's okay, so off they go.

April 20—LST 491

The executive officer appears much pleased with my gang of men, and well he ought to be, too! They've been leaning into their work with a spirit that's wonderful. The pruning and discarding I've done in the past 2 months is bearing fruit, and the quality of the men under me is higher than I've ever enjoyed before.

I sent out the sketch pads today, snooks. Won't be long before they reach you, I hope. No mail for any of our outfit today, so maybe

The Executive Officer, LST 491

The crew, LST 491

tomorrow we'll make connections. Am dying for dope on your apartment! I'll mark time till I hear from you.

April 23—LST 491

Seven p.m. in the evening, and a real busy Sunday it's been too. Tommy showed me the letter you wrote him. Thanks so much. You're the sweetest thing God ever made, Junie. Why you should trifle with this sailor is more than I'll ever understand.

Living on this margin, where values and standards are such impersonal entities, where "important" things are so temporal, where "people" stop and "jobs" start, where worth is synonymous with "efficiency" rather than the ability to harness dreams and make them so. Such existence is completely negative, so terribly foreign to that which we've fashioned for ourselves, June. You are the reason that only half of me can be regimented. The other half goes on dreaming. I have this most sincere regret that every man here doesn't have his June back home, preserving the sparks, mothering the fire of sensitivity and softness that these cold men will need so desperately. Humanity needs love and warmth, even as it does sacrifice.

April 29—LST 491

This has been the longest intermission in our letters since I left the States, and I hope that it hasn't upset or worried you. It's impossible to explain it until I'm with you again, sweetheart. Suffice for now to tell you I've been working exceedingly hard and long—and you understand any break in my letters is caused externally and not by the promptings of a lazy or indifferent heart. For I've wanted so much to talk with you this last week, Junie, wanted it with all my heart.

Opposite:
Bo'sun's mate, LST 491

Such are the fortunes of men at war. No bitter commentary can change them. Their complete indifference to human values is frighteningly monstrous, and the enormity of their movements makes one guy's destiny a frail shadow in their wake. The feeling comes eventually to everyone over here, I think. Your complete impotence and inability to alter one iota of what is and what will be. It evolves at last to doing your job, staying where you should be, and praying for the future. If we seem callous, it will be from our experience in living where our genius, our talents, our control over what is or what will be, has been shrunk to insignificance by events that move unwilled, and to all but a very few, unexplained and unmastered. You learn to accept "what is to be is to be" as your own. But it's so foreign to us Americans. We're bred from infancy to feel that "there it is, pick it up, shape it, mold it." Its only reason for being there is so you could make it your own. It's your life. But that's not here, any of it.

One very nice thing happened to me this week. One day early in the week, the men and Badger and I really went to town. We sweated blood from 7:15 in the morning until 9 at night. The men worked like hell, and we accomplished a week's work on the boats. We were all completely bushed. The men went down to their quarters and I went to the wardroom for a cup of coffee. At 10 p.m., the first lieutenant came to me and

told me of a work detail that had to be done before morning. I hated like hell to tell the men, but I had to. I went down to their quarters and found ten of them already in the sacks asleep. The others were about to go in. So I told them the situation and said I was going down to the tank deck to start the work myself. If any of them would like to join me they'd be damn welcome. I left them and went below. In three minutes' time every one of those tired kids was down there with me. It was a wonderful feeling, darling. They've done a swell job since they've been aboard.

Hope the sketchbooks have found their way to you. The men and officers are needling me for portraits to "send to my wife." I dodge one and run smack into another. But it's a great feeling to keep turning out something—anything.

D-DAY was going to be very soon. We all felt it. The weather was right for it. It had to be. So any chance for a leave from the ship felt like a pardon now. Spring was happening in the hills above Salcombe, and the lockstep routines of shipboard life felt unbearably confining. So when it was my turn for leave, I'd stuff a duffel bag with some shirts and sketch pads, salute the flag and the officer of the deck, go swiftly down the gangplank, and start to breathe again.

May 11—England (on leave)

These past few days have been kind of strange—not bad, just kind of sweet and sad. I've been doing a lot of dreaming, probably in part caused by the beauty and loveliness of this bit of England we're seeing now. It's incredibly graceful—defying description.

There's a magic in this English spring for me that is tender and sweetly melancholy-feeling, almost like an Indian summer back home. Strange that in all this gorgeous pattern of dancing fragrance and lush greens and rebirth in the earth there should be this autumnal sadness that seems to come from its very beauty. And yet the wonder of the renascence is there in the whispering of the buds, in every movement of these scented winds. But there is something stirring, uneasy, restless in it all. Maybe it's the intrusion of these great pounding, arrogant bloodhounds of war. That's my spring, beloved Junie, sad and beautiful, bittersweet, full of promise, and an impatient sense of loss.

Horror story of the week. Tommy sent Helen a letter written to Wendy, and Wendy a letter written to Helen! It's too terrible to contemplate. Meanwhile, Tommy is keeping in touch with his English acquisition from our last land base. No comment.

May 16—LST 491

It's 11:45 and I'm sleepy, but I want to write you a bit anyhow. This is a most dreadful situation and I don't know what to do about it. As of May 1st, we've been told, no mail has left the country for the States. No mail will leave until further notice. I received five wonderful letters from you today and noted that the last one of mine you received was sent out April 29. I'm afraid that will be the last you receive for a while, although I've kept on writing. I know somehow that you feel I'm all right.

Don't let the incessant commentators and sensation mongers touch your mind and spirit, Junie. I can sense the growing tension and anxiety in your heart. It's no wonder. While we here are almost oblivious to news, developments, prognostications, you're enmeshed in them. This fever that is growing in the States is felt somehow by all of us here. Living here each day is completely unemotional. You're too busy doing your work with your men or your matériel to indulge in this psychological war dance that is increasing in tempo at home. Keep cool. It's just a job I must and want to do. I count on your common sense and sound values as I do on my own aptitude, training, and ability. Together, we can lick this thing to a frazzle.

May 17—LST 491

Honest to Pete, I get so goddamned aggravated. There isn't a single second of privacy to be had, nor a single moment when you can say, This is my time. Leave me alone. It's a series of interruptions, little annoying interruptions, running somewhere for something for somebody. I'm just up to my ears with it!

Happily, I get no time to stew in my own juice. I'm not being paid to enjoy this job, just to do it. Like everything else in the world, you have to pay for what you get—for the thrill of putting on this uniform for the first time back at Notre Dame midshipman school, for the pride and satisfaction of being a naval officer. You pay and pay in inconvenience, drudgery, repetition, and responsibility. It's a debt that never gets paid. You hope for the respect of your superiors and the affection of your men. But the job itself is the important thing.

May 20—LST 491

This spring of '44 will be engraved on my mind. What a strange and terrible time this is. Someday our kids will read in school about the spring of '44, and it will be dusty and meaningless to them. Yet how very vivid and momentous to live through it. To see the weight, to sense the power, to speculate on where, when, how—to be a tiny, insignificant, and almost meaningless part of it all—and yet to have so much at stake in the game. You've placed your bet and somebody else is rolling the dice. For you, it's the works—your whole wad—and yet you know that yours is a side bet. The stakes stagger your imagination. But you don't worry about it! That's the wonderful and incongruous thing. Why not? Maybe you just can't picture losing. Maybe the job immediately to be done looms so large it throws the main show into shadow. You can black out the sun with your hand.

June 1—LST 491

Hope this gets out to you. It'll be the last word from me for a long time. DON'T WORRY. I'm feeling wonderfully well and absolutely squared away for anything that may come my way. For this wonderful peace of mind, I have you to thank, Junie. Please call folks and tell them I'm fine but can't write them. Bye for a little, angel. Remember I love you with all my heart always.

D-DAY

THE INVASION

THE LAST MEN from the liberty party had just returned in the LCVP from Salcombe. The small assault boat rose up and crashed down with each swell that raced across the harbor. Soaked with spray and still high from their liberty ashore, the men were laughing, shouting obscene instructions to the coxswain as he wrestled to keep his craft flush with the cargo net that dangled from the deck of our LST.

"You're ruining my dress blues, you bastard! Can't you drive this mother?"

The voices from the boat were nearly lost in the rising wind. I watched the sailors gauge the moment when the bucking assault boat would rise on the wave. With a loud whoop, they'd lunge for the cargo net, catch hold and scramble up to the deck. They saluted the officer of the deck and the flag, and were making their raucous way to their quarters when the ship's loudspeaker suddenly chattered.

"Now hear this. All shore leave is canceled. All hands are to remain aboard. All officers proceed to the wardroom." The sailors stopped and stared at the loudspeaker. "The ship is sealed."

"Let's get this boat up," I said to my small-boat crew. We dropped the cables to the pitching LCVP, the coxswain secured them, and the winch eased the dripping boat toward its position on the waiting davit. But as the LST rolled in the choppy Channel water, the LCVP swung out on the cables and then crashed against the side of the ship.

"Christ!" I thought. "These are the boats I've sweated to equip for the invasion!" I was frantic that they not get crippled now. Together we struggled to strap the swinging boat into place, and finally secured it to the davit. "Good job, men!" I said, and trotted across the deck to the wardroom. "Ship is sealed," I thought. "It's got to be D-Day!"

The skipper looked carefully around the crowded room. "Are we all here? Good. Okay, gentlemen. It's time to unseal the orders and find out what we're supposed to do."

He unrolled the package of charts on the wardroom table. For hours we studied the voluminous intelligence data about what was waiting across the Channel. There were silhouettes of the Cotentin Peninsula, breakdowns of what German units were entrenched behind the dunes. There were names of their commanders and the percentages of what ethnic groups were in each outfit. And most important to all of us, the specific transport areas ten miles off the Normandy coast where the cruisers, battleships, transports, and supply ships would converge; and the assault area closer in, where the

LSTs from all the ports along the English Channel would rendezvous. From the assault area, we could see the "Mason-Dixon line" where the LCVPs were to await their signal to race to the fortified beaches.

There were descriptions of enemy armor and what air support was in place behind the beaches. There were warnings of magnetized mines and deadly hedgehogs that had been placed to snag our assault craft. And there were pictures of "Rommel's spaghetti," the lethal pointed poles that had been planted in fields and marshes to disable Allied gliders and destroy any assaults from the air. We were exhilarated that so much intelligence had been done to guarantee success. And we saw for the first time what our objective was. It was a sector called Uncle Red on a beach called Utah.

After all the tedium, the endless dry runs and practice landings, after all the night watches in the German U-boat-infested Channel, the waiting was about to end. Tomorrow—June 5! For five years the British and the Russians had kept us from losing. Now it was our turn to win it. D-Day!

The meeting in the wardroom ended and a few of us lingered, too wound up to be alone. Someone turned on the radio, and there was the teasing, seductive voice of Axis Sally.

"Hello, Yanks. Are you ever coming? Oh, do come. We'll be waiting. See you at the Mason-Dixon line."

The Mason-Dixon line! Jesus Christ, they knew about the Mason-Dixon line? We simply stared at each other.

The storm that started on June 4 kept building in intensity. The LSTs across Salcombe harbor rolled wildly. As I came off watch at midnight, I checked the small boats and all seemed secure. I looked

Opposite:
A wardroom meeting

across at the ships in our flotilla and was startled to see a thick gray cloud of fog settle on the roiling water. One by one, the ships were blotted from sight. I headed for my quarters and determined to sleep fast.

At 0500, a sailor roused me. "Skipper wants to see his small-boat officers. Says you and Mr. Buttabaugh are to report to the bridge immediately."

When I came out on deck, the bow of my ship was not visible in the damn soup. There was a muffled slap of lines against the mast as the ship rolled silently back and forth. The skipper was reading a dispatch as we entered the bridge. He nodded briefly. "We've got new orders. This damn storm has fouled everything up. The whole operation has been set back twenty-four hours. D-Day will be tomorrow, the sixth. SHAEF hopes the storm will abate by then." He stared morosely through the glass. "We've got to notify the ships in our flotilla about the delay. The fog's so thick we can't signal them. So take your boats around the harbor and pass the word, ship by ship. They're all standing by, waiting to go. It won't be easy. It's damn thick out there."

As we dropped from the davits to the water below, the sides of our own ship became only a dirty swatch of darker gray, then disappeared as we made our careful way to the ships hidden in the silent fog. As we'd edge alongside, we'd call up to the officer of the deck. "New orders from the 491. We're not sailing today. We go tomorrow." High overhead we heard the sodden beat of a bomber squadron. Heading out? Heading back? Soon all was silent again and we returned to our ship to wait one more time.

The skipper told us that only one small-boat officer would make

Opposite:
Amphibious officers, LST 491

Waiting for D-Day

the invasion. He'd be assigned to Utah Beach and remain until further orders reached him. The other small-boat officer would remain with the ship and would make the invasion in the south of France. "You decide among yourselves who goes," he said. Danny Buttabaugh and I flipped a coin. I won Normandy and my fate was sealed. For the next six months, every waking hour was to be spent on Utah Beach. Some of it would be very rough duty. Buttabaugh had seemingly won the easier assignment.

I WOKE AS THE 491 cleared Salcombe harbor early in the morning of June 6. I glanced at my watch and realized that one hundred and thirty-five miles across the Channel the first assault wave was already coming under the guns of the German shore batteries. The fog had blown away, and a bright sun glittered on the water. Our ship was in a long column of LSTs, each one rising and dipping on the long swells left from the storm. All the army personnel were topside. Some men nervously cleaned their rifles, while others checked the vehicles which were chained to the deck. Clusters of soldiers and sailors gathered at the rail, staring out at the endless armada that began to build in our wake. Only the engineering crew was missing the pageant as they sweated in the bowels of the ship.

Ahead of us were patrol craft, minesweepers, and guide boats, plowing through the chill wind and hard chop of the Channel. Behind us now was every description of landing craft, each loaded with men and matériel. As we shadowed the English coastline heading east, we were joined by more and more craft from every little harbor that had been our practice homes for the last five months. The drone of aircraft was a steady din. P-47s and P-51s shepherded the fleets of bombers as they bisected our caravan, heading due south. The whole world seemed to be assembling, and we felt we were part of an irresistible juggernaut.

As the sun reached its zenith, the patrol craft leading the LSTs wheeled to starboard. The ships now headed due south. Dead ahead, through binoculars, we could make out the smudge of land that was Normandy. Somewhere on the pale strip of sand and dune was Uncle Red, our sector of Utah Beach. I said a silent prayer and went to check my small boats. My boat crews were at their stations, and when the order came we lowered the boats from their davits.

It was slow going as the army men made their way down the cargo net into the LCVPs. They were loaded down with rifles, gas masks, and bundles of gear. Even in the stiff wind that was still kicking up the Channel, there was a foul stench from our gas-repellent coveralls. Mixed with the smell of brine, it made every stomach queasy. "There's a fifty-fifty chance the Krauts will hit us with gas on the beach," we were told. "Wear coveralls and keep your mask dry."

For the next three hours, we circled off Utah Beach, waiting for our signal to move. It was miserable going. The seas were unrelenting, hitting our tiny craft on the bow and then amidships as we'd turn. The diesel exhaust of the laboring boats mixed with the odor of vomit from seasick soldiers. The crew and I struggled to keep on station, praying for the lights on the patrol craft to turn green so we could head to shore. To the left, I could make out the beachhead of Omaha Beach, a long sloping strand running to a cliff. What I thought were piles of cordwood at the base of the cliff, I learned later were the bodies of twenty-five hundred men, killed by withering fire from the Nazi gun emplacements built into the cliff.

Five miles out in the Channel were the cruisers and battleships that were the heavy artillery of our attack. The reverberating roar of their 12- and 16-inch guns echoed across the water. Every time the huge shells passed overhead, we would flinch. It felt as if streetcars were being hurled at the beaches. A steady muted murmur came from the distant beach as waves of dive-bombers tore through the low clouds and smoke, dropping their bombs on the fortified bunkers above the beach.

Finally the green light flashed from the patrol crafts, and we began to edge toward shore. The sun was beginning to descend when we finally reached Uncle Red. Many of the sand dunes beyond the long shallow beachhead were shrouded in smoke. As it drifted to sea, it hid the lethal hedgehogs that had blown up many of the boats in the early waves of the assault. Slowly and carefully we made our way through the maze of torn iron and shattered hulks, straining to see any floating mines that might still lie in wait. The stink of cordite and rubber from burning vehicles fouled the air.

Stretching off to the east, Utah Beach was a deadly tapestry of chaos and carnage. LCVPs were continuing to thread their way toward the beach, where they would drop their ramps and release the weary and ashen-faced soldiers. Whenever a German 88 shell exploded on the beach, the soldiers would attempt to run through the surf, sagging with the sodden weight of their gear. Desperately they searched the nightmarish clutter of the beach, looking for their outfits. Up and down the beach, fires continued to burn. The boom of detonating mines made us wince as the minesweepers just off the beachhead continued to patrol the flanks of the invasion force.

We landed our troops as dusk began to cloak the eastern end of

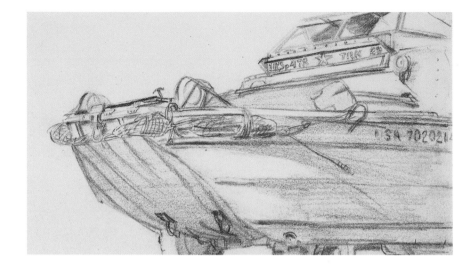

An amphibious "duck"

Utah Beach. Once our boat ramp hit the sand the weary soldiers ran out onto the cluttered beach. I followed them down the ramp, pulled by an odd longing to step onto French soil after so many endless months of waiting. But I didn't linger. The light was fading fast, and I soon lost sight of the men we'd landed as they raced toward the protection of a sand dune.

"Let's get the hell out of here while we can still see," I told the crews. As the coxswains warily edged off the beach, I watched an LCT, a much larger vessel than ours, pull itself off the sand and head slowly out to the safer water beyond the mined hell of the beach-head. "Follow right behind him," I told my coxswains, "but not too close. He can run interference for us!" By the time the LCT had dropped its hook, darkness covered Utah Beach. Only the sullen glow of the still burning wreckage indicated the part of the darkness where the war had come ashore.

We tied up alongside the LCT and got permission to sleep on its deck. Tracers of artillery curved high above us, and the boat shivered from the distant thud of explosions. We were exhausted and we were exultant. Christ! We had survived D-Day! I smiled in the dark, thought of June, and incredibly, fell asleep.

We woke to a roaring that startled us. As we scrambled to our feet, the first of a long column of C-47s filled the sky over our heads. They seemed to skim the masts of the invasion craft huddled off the still smoldering beachhead. Behind each plane was a wide-winged glider filled with troops. As they passed the beachhead, the C-47s released the gliders. In a moment they were lost in the haze that hung like a shroud over the dunes. As we ate our C rations, wave after wave of planes and gliders lumbered above us on the run into Sector Red. "Eat up," I said. "There's a war going on over there." We climbed into our boats and headed for the beach. And we found our war.

FOR THE NEXT WEEKS, time ceased to have a measured cadence. Mornings, afternoons, evenings, and nighttimes simply imploded in a jumble of action and exhaustion. We worked until we couldn't work any longer. When we'd stop, we'd cadge food and bed down on the deck of a friendly ship, waiting to hit the beach at the first tide. Then we'd start again, carrying ammo, hauling the injured out to the hospital ships, running urgent messages out to the command cruiser offshore. Our little LCVPs were constantly in demand, diesel-spewing conduits for everything that seemed to be desperately needed. All these decades later, just the rank smell of the diesel exhaust of a New York City bus triggers memories of those frantic days in our little boats. A scrim of time seems to soften the raw visual images. What is remembered indelibly is the smell, the weariness, and the painful frustration at one's feeble capacities to make the tiniest difference. Yet a few mental snapshots remain vividly alive.

NORMANDY

ON UTAH BEACH

THE LONG, SHALLOW STRAND that was Utah Beach allowed the invasion craft to come far up on the sand at high tide. The ramps of the LCTs and the great bow doors of the LSTs would crank open, and out would pour the men and myriad matériel needed to feed the furnaces of the front lines. If the disgorging of the ships took too long, they would sit on the beach like stranded whales, their crews nervously scanning the skies for enemy aircraft and counting the hours till they could be released again by the incoming tide. As the terriers who served their needs, our little LCVPs were also often held hostage by a swiftly retreating tide.

On D+3, my boats were naked on the beach. Our last run had finished after dark, and we were exhausted. My men and I welcomed the break in the frantic schedule, and the hours waiting for the returning tide seemed like a stolen holiday. The men were relaxing in the boat, reading comic books and napping. I lounged against the

A moment to rest

plywood stern on the sand, gazing idly up the beach as the sun began to drop to the west.

The German came right out of the sun, his engine roaring and his guns blazing. I blinked hard at the unbelievable image and then screamed to the men in the boats, "Get down! Get down!" The Messerschmitt zigzagged his way down the beach, heading toward our boats. I threw myself behind my plywood boat into a huge puddle. My steel helmet went rolling across the sand as I cringed, waiting for the bullets to hit me. "Stay down! Stay down!" I yelled, as I heard wood shattering on the boat above my head.

Now all hell broke loose. Every ship waiting on the tide opened fire at the Messerschmitt as it dodged and wove its way down the beach. The roar of the plane faded, and I could hear the yells of the men dug in on the dunes. "They got him! They got him!" I raised my head from the puddle and saw the plane, trailing smoke, as it disappeared beyond the seawall. I stared at the ribbon of holes tattooed on the boat above my head and scrambled to my feet.

"Are you guys all right?" I yelled up to the boat, fearing that my crew was dead.

Silence. Finally a small voice called out, "We're scared shit. But the bastard missed us!"

I laughed with relief. "You can get up now. The tide's coming in."

YOU CAN GO TO WAR and never see the guys that run it. I never met an admiral. And the only time I met a general, I didn't mean to. On D+1 we started to organize the chaos left from the initial assault of D-Day. It was bedlam, a cacophony of roarings and rattlings and screaming winches. It was the clanking of tanks and the groaning of bulldozers as the Seabees tore out the sand to build a causeway for all the armor that was panting to come ashore. It was the braying of sergeants and the pounding of huge hammers to build the stockades for the German prisoners who had surrendered. It was the shouting of orders as latrines were dug and aid stations cut into the dunes behind the beach. And there were the constant calls for our boats: "We got wounded…We got dead…We got ammo…" When I returned from still one more run out to the command vessel, three sailors who were extracting a dead soldier from an upended LCM called to me. "Can you find the burial detail?" I told them I'd try. When we ground to a halt on the sand, I ran up to a group of soldiers at the base of a sand dune. Breathless, I grabbed the shoulder of the nearest GI and said, "Are you the burial detail?"

The man turned, and I saw the single star on his helmet. "No, son," he said quietly. "I'm not the burial detail." He smiled at my confusion and pointed down the beach. "I think you'll find them near the causeway." The general turned back to the war, and I swiftly cleared the area.

I CAN'T EVEN IMAGINE how many guns there were on the ships that unloaded every day on Utah Beach. There were troop ships, Liberty ships, and every variety of navy craft bringing cargo or protecting the staggering herd that arrived at each new tide. In the early days of the beachhead, every nerve ending on every member of every gun crew seemed tautly "at the ready" as they searched the skies for marauders. It became an excruciating drama to witness. When a German plane came barreling out of the clouds, some kid with a .30-caliber machine gun would open up. His shots would trigger gun crews across the entire beachhead. A barrage of fire would erupt, often destroying the German plane and, tragically, the pursuing Allied plane as well. On more than one occasion, I witnessed the startled pursuer pull up to avoid the fire, waggling his wings to identify himself as an American or Brit, and then get shot down by the trigger-happy gun crews.

On D+10, a furious British flyer was brought in a jeep to my boat. "I want to see the son of a bitch who's in charge of this sector!" he demanded.

"Yes, sir," I responded. "He's out there on the command ship. I'll take you out to meet him."

On the long ride out to the cruiser, the aviator told me his story. "In the last ten days, I've been shot down in three bloody planes over this bloody beach!" I delivered the man to the ship and wished him good luck. "Good luck? Three fucking planes!" he growled, and strode up the gangway.

One hour later, the command ship flashed an urgent message to all ships in the area. "You are not—repeat, not—to begin firing at any aircraft until this command authorizes it. If this is not immediately observed, all air cover for Utah Beach will be removed. Repeat: All air cover for Utah Beach will be removed." In the next six months, I never saw another Allied plane shot down over Utah Beach.

IN THE EARLY DAYS of the Utah beachhead, I noticed a remarkable phenomenon. Sailors and soldiers would be noisily busy with their building, carrying, constructing, unloading—a wild choreography of movement that ranged as far as the eye could see. Whenever a deadly German 88 artillery shell would explode on the beach, there would be a sudden hush and stasis. Then every sailor would bolt seaward for the shelter of a ship, and every soldier would race to the nearest foxhole in the dune.

On one occasion, I had left my men and boats at the temporary causeway and moved up the beach for a repair tool I needed. Halfway there, an 88 exploded, sending its shower of rocks and sand in the air, and sending me sprawling on the sand. I realized that the tide was too far out to allow me to scramble to the nearest ship. Before another shell could land, I climbed to my feet and raced for the nearest sand dune. Spotting a foxhole, I threw myself headlong into it. Unfortunately, two GIs had gotten there first, and I landed on their backs. Cursing, they brushed wet sand from their faces and stared at me. "For Crissakes, sailor! Go find yourself a ship!" With no dignity at all, I untangled myself from the sodden foxhole and ran the hundreds of yards to the nearest navy vessel. Home, I reflected, is where the heart is.

IN THE MIDDLE OF A WAR, there is no time for reflection, and no time for letters home. It would be a while, a long while, before I sorted out the many emotions that flashed through me during our assault of Utah Beach. The overwhelming impulse is to get the job done and get out of there. But a month or so later, I did tell June some of what I was feeling in the aftermath of battle.

July 25—Utah Beach

If I were king in America, I would start every radio program with, "Don't go to sleep, America." I'd have every front page carry a banner headline seven days a week that says, "Nothing is over but the shouting." I'd sell them peace whether they liked all it means or not. I'd teach them responsibility as absolutely as they taught their kids how to kill other kids. I'd teach them that war is a social disease bred on the filth of bigotry and stupidity.

I'd show them this war as the manifestation of moral infection and that our part was the surgery necessary—not the infection itself. I can't believe, Junie, that men will always have to fight. Men don't always have to fight. They detest it. And if they didn't when they came, they learned to damn quickly. I believe with all my heart there must be a finality this time. I pray to God that someone, anyone, will take the lead and save a score of generations from the shame and disgust of winning and losing the same war again.

But that was in July. This is the first letter I wrote home after the invasion.

June 12 (D+6)—Somewhere off France

Darling Junie, I hope that long before you get this note you will have received the cable I gave to one of the officers who was returning to England, and know that I'm perfectly ok. I used mental telepathy real hard and kind of had a hunch that you were tuning in! I'm swell darlin'—honest to Pete!

I find that this "invasion" stuff is nothing more nor less than a hell of a lot of work. The excitement is spotted through it, but is the exception, not the rule. Today is D plus 6, about an entire week since we hit the beach. You can't stay excited that long. You get much too concerned wondering where the devil you're going to find a sack, and who will feed you, and where you can shave. After a bit, the unusual and dangerous elements fall into place. I've seen a good deal. We weren't in the assault landings, but got there very late that day.

When I see you again I'll whisper all the sordid details into your ears. But for now all I can tell you is that you are still the possessor of one unspoiled, lonesome, dirty husband. I have two crews, two boats, and orders temporarily detaching me from the 491 for duty with the other small-boat men operating around this area. This is the first real break I've gotten, and I've actually got time to sit down and write.

I've been working with Tommy Wolfe and the "revival meeting" lads from Fowey. They're a swell bunch. The news we get seems encouraging, but it's fragmentary, mostly scraps picked up from different men coming back out from the lines. You probably know a great deal more than me. It's been something to see, believe me, Junie.

I'm going through the process now of shaking down all the sensations and sights I've felt and seen, and trying to figure out my relation to the whole setup. I think I've reached a couple of conclusions so far. First: that my respect for the average Joe in the army is unlimited. Too much can't be said about him. He's tough, courageous, and just as commonplace as hell. He's self-contained and pretty damn wonderful. The sailors, of course, aren't exposed to the furnace in the same way, but they're good kids. The pettiness and smallness you hate in them on shipboard disappeared when they got into their job. The American kid is a pretty level-headed guy, and his sense of humor goes on ticking no matter what.

I don't think I was scared. If I was, it wasn't at all the kind of fright I had imagined. There were a couple of times that things happened around me. At the time you are just too busy and excited to figure out whether you're frightened. When you look back on it, you get the willies!

I've been thinking so much about you, Junie. I pray that you kept that wonderful chin up and held on tight until you heard from me. I'm ok—fit, healthy, and loving you something fierce.

June 13—Utah Beach

These past seven days have been filled with sights and sounds I'll probably recall always. Most of the invasion was pretty exciting, a lot of it pretty nasty, none of it enjoyable. Through it all and leading up to our hitting the beach, there must have been—looking back now—a certain growing tension in all of us, a great deal of self-searching. For myself—looking back now—I found I was completely set for anything. There was a completeness and reason in my living up to that point that was answer in itself. Above all, I prayed that I would live to make you happy. I wanted to live. Living has always been like a new toy for me. And I wanted to live with you, and for you.

June 14—Utah Beach

Nuther day just ending, a pretty bright one, but kind of lonely. Seems to be a chronic ailment of late. Must be born of the reaction—the sudden poignant awareness of it. Somehow every day of our being apart was rationalized into one more unit toward the invasion. The invasion was the tall wall at the end of the street. Every step was one nearer to it, every action designed to jump the obstacle. Now, quite suddenly, the wall is jumped, and there is still a ways to the corner. Time has suddenly slowed to a walk. Where days raced by almost unnoticed but a few days ago, the hours are suddenly pushing forward and baring their 60 teeth. I'm still in the green coveralls I've been wearing since D-Day, and this morning I took my first bath since the invasion!

June 18—Utah Beach

I bitch a lot, but don't let the bitching worry you, please. Without bitching, this whole setup would be impossible. After all, bitching is just rebellious impatience at the status quo. And the world's greatest bitchers are those who, having known the best before, are discontent until it's theirs again. I choose to include myself in this category.

We are still working off this craft, an LCI (landing craft, infantry). I haven't seen our mama ship since D plus 2. Everything I own is still aboard her except three pairs of shorts and T-shirts, two sets of coveralls, and two pairs of socks. Have no funds nohow, but that doesn't matter 'cause there's no place to spend it. In this area, there is nothing of France for the navy men except sandy beaches. We live aboard ship and are forbidden to go inland. We keep running our taxi service between the ships. Our future remains uncertain.

June 27—Utah Beach

Today we got Cherbourg! A <u>wonderful</u> victory. We need more and we'll get them!

I am somewhat permanently settled, and I may be out of small boats. Real involved, but the long and short of it is that small-boat crews have been sent back to England. Their officers have remained here, myself included. It seems that we are severing relations with small boats. I'm trying to make myself indispensable aboard this

transport (the T. B. Robertson) that I've been on for the past two days. If I can, I'll be doing a job aboard ship. It's certainly worth a gamble, and I'm going to play it for all it's worth. Small-boat personnel are the most neglected element in the navy, and I'm not eager to grow old in an open small boat. My new resolution is to get the hell out of it. So, for the moment, I'm living aboard a very civilized ship.

M Y WISH TO FIND A BERTH on the port direction ship, the *T. B. Robertson*, was happily realized. For the first time in weeks, I knew where I would sleep. The *Robertson* was an American freighter, a Liberty ship. She carried a merchant marine crew and had quarters built in the ship's holds for the navy personnel who would work as part of the port direction team. My new duty was to be the hydrographic officer for Utah Beach, mapping those areas of the Channel that had been swept free from the deadly German mines that had been sown before the invasion. In addition, I was to help guide the daily ship traffic from England to safe berths off the beach. It was a fascinating vantage point from which to observe the growing and awesome power of the invasion force that was retaking Europe. In a more personal vein, my new duties meant I could sometimes steal "downtime" to assess what was happening around and to me, and for continuing my sketches and paintings for forward shipment to my eager wife.

Opposite:
The merchant marine
crew aboard the
T. B. Robertson

Overleaf:
Hold #1—Officers' quarters
on the Robertson

One of my "kids"

June 28—T. B. Robertson

I do think the "throes of war" have left me quite unscathed physically and mentally. I do not feel "older than my years" nor "hardened by the crucible of fire." Nothing I've seen has changed anything fundamentally in me. Possibly my resolution has sharpened some, my enthusiasm slightly tempered, my tolerance and understanding somewhat broadened. I think that's happened to most of us in some degree.

Being here, there has had to be an assertion of self and an independent spirit. If these are bounded by humility and a decent memory of what actually was, then it should be a healthy influence, not a corruption. For living with these men and these officers day in and day out is a conditioning in tolerance and selflessness that is a paradoxical product of such an insanity as war. Such a thing as intolerance or prejudice simply does not exist here, for it's not real but superficial. I shall never accept graciously any prejudice that I encounter when I get home. Those things of which we talked for so long, Junie, are all so terribly true. I've only seen intolerance when men were more comfortable and sitting back, relaxed again. When we were on the beaches, you never heard the loose talk of "niggers" you once heard in the wardrooms. Then the very men who were ducking bullets with the colored lads only weeks before would revert to the comfortable bigotry they had known before. As for religious intolerance, it's never been an issue here. How sad a commentary it is that the men have to leave their most abundant lives and their organized houses of religion before they become aware of their sameness. When organization is forgotten and the message is remembered, you don't find words like "Kike" entering the conversation.

July 1—T. B. Robertson

There are those long twilights here now. The sky is billions of miles away, and you feel very much alone. The water stretches away forever—no waves, hardly a ripple. The ships sit alone in the water, each in its own pool of aloneness. The sky arcs up from millions of miles beyond the shore. And straight up there's nothing. It's big and empty and very quiet. The sun goes away, and it's still too big, too light. The emptiness comes off the water and crawls right into you.

July 5—Normandy

The news is good. The Russians are past Minsk and going strong. And the sun has been shining almost continually. For the little things, Lord, we are truly thankful. Yesterday was kind of a punk Fourth of July. Everyone was thinking too much of home and feeling sorry for himself. Like me, for instance. Last night, just as dusk started creeping across the water, the kids on the ships about (without any plan or signal beforehand) started to fire off the Very pistols and flares from the pyrotechnic boxes of each ship. It was ironic and a little sad. The reds and yellows and whites and greens danced like fire on the water. And then it was too dark and the men went to their sacks. I don't imagine it was a very happy Fourth anywhere this year.

Tonight I saw the first woman I've seen since before the invasion. It felt good just to look at her. She was a nurse on a hospital ship, and I'll be damned if I know if she was pretty or not. But after five weeks without even seeing a skirt, the crew and I just stared and waved like the bald-headed row up front at the burlesque!

July 10—Normandy

This afternoon I went ashore for the first time in over a fortnight. Hopped on a mail truck going inland for a ways—way way back of the front lines but still off the beaches, which had so far constituted the greater part of my impressions of La Belle France. We stopped a couple of miles inland in one of the little towns. It was here that I saw my first French civilians—some little kids quite scrubbed, a few old people on bikes. Some of them waved and most of them smiled. The kids were like kids all over! Occasionally you saw a two-wheeled cart clopping along the road alongside the jeeps and the trucks and then you were conscious again that you were in a farmers' country as well as a theater of operations.

The mail center was at a lovely old home, a chateau I guess, that the Krauts had used for the past couple of years. I wandered around the grounds and into the garage, where a couple of boys were tinkering with a car. One of them was a handsome kid who spoke good English and turned out to be part of the family who owned the home. He led me into the part of the home where the family still lives and introduced me to his mother, a lovely sweet old woman, who spoke a little English and even in those cramped quarters was the perfect hostess. She put a beautiful bouquet of garden flowers on the table and broke out a bottle of dry wine which was delicious. "Vive la France" and "Vive l'Amérique!" They liked us fine and they didn't like the Jerries nohow. It was a fine afternoon!

Tonight I asked my boss if I might get a few days off in England so I might get my gear, orders, and mail rounded up. He said it was okay with him, but I must get permission from higher authorities on the beach. So tomorrow I'm gonna take a crack at it, pooch. Nothing ventured, nothing gained.

BY THIS TIME, the clothes I'd brought with me from England were tattered and too dirty to ever be clean again. Desperate for some decent gear, I begged the port director of Utah Beach for orders that could get me back to England. When I returned to my old base at Fowey to recover the clothes I had left behind, I was hailed by the chaplain, a man named Walkup. "Tracy, you're back, Lord be praised! Come on in, come right on in!" I followed him into the Quonset hut and watched as he reached into his footlocker and extracted a wrapped present. On the wrapping it said, "Merry Christmas, Tracy."

"I've kept this for you for just this occasion, but you're back a little early." The chaplain was from Kentucky, had a native's deep appreciation of good bourbon, and presented me with a wonderful bottle of Jack Daniel's. We had become friends when I sang with his small choral group at Sunday services at Fowey. I was touched by his thoughtfulness, and I insisted that we baptize the Jack Daniel's on this very happy reunion. "I always loved your hymn 'Brighten the Corner Where You Are,'" I said. And we did so.

My leave from Utah Beach to retrieve my gear permitted me enough time to visit London, a city I had longed to see. When I checked into the Grosvenor Hotel late in the morning, the housemaid was still making up the bed. I told her to take her time because I was going out immediately to see the city. Our conversation was interrupted by the sound of a motor, which was swiftly getting louder, the noise filling the room. I hurried to the window and leaned out, spotting what appeared to be a small, wingless plane. As I watched it pass, the motor stopped abruptly and the object dove towards the ground, disappearing behind the clustered houses of a square. There was an immediate huge explosion. Startled, I turned to see the maid cautiously emerging from under my bed.

"What was that?" I asked the ashen-faced young woman.

She stared at me. "You don't know, sir? Crimey, that was a buzz bomb—a V-1 rocket. They are very awful. And if I may say so, you must never ever go to a window when you hear one!"

Shaken, I could only nod in affirmation. A V-1 rocket! "Christ," I thought, "I got through D-Day without a scratch. And now I can get blown up on leave in the middle of London!"

I thanked the young woman for her good advice, and cautiously went out of the hotel to see the great city. A dark pall of smoke was rising from a neighborhood only two blocks away, and I could hear the Klaxons of the emergency vehicles racing to the scene. But the Londoners on the street continued their conversations as they strolled to their offices or lunch. "Unflappable people," I thought.

July 19—England

The leave is just about over, and nothing remains except a nice feeling. I've lost that uncomfortable sense of drifting around sans clothes, mail, etc. I'm taking my sketchbook back with me, hon, and that too should help

I haven't sketched in a hell of a while, and I think even if I had the materials with me, I would have done very little. D-Day and the days after were not conducive to the old creative instinct. There was a hesitant, negative atmosphere, and too much positive horror and revulsion for a guy to sit and calmly record it. Someday maybe I'll get some of it on paper, but I couldn't then.

I'm purposely aware of any changes in myself because I'm

curious to know what it's going to be like meeting you again and everyone back home. I feel a little older and even a little wiser, and I'm quite pleased that I've been where I have been. It's not a matter of conceit—I had to be there, whether I wanted to or not—but rather a feeling that I've been through the mill and have seen more than enough. Somehow I feel now that I've paid for my ticket. I have no illusions about being a hero or being tough. Because I am neither. But there is a certain satisfaction in having been there. I feel a little more confident and a little more sure.

July 21—T. B. Robertson

A rainy, gray, nasty day today. The only sunshine was the news that somebody went after Schicklgruber and FDR was renominated.

Y'know, I get the shakes every time I think about starting on a portfolio. I wonder what I'll want to do when I get back. Unlike the child who steps into a toy store and immediately wants everything, I seem to discard everything. It's not a matter of looking down my nose at these guys that are knocking out the stuff they're reproducing. Some of it I think is fine, some of it excellent—but none of it makes me jealous that I didn't do it. I can't imagine anything duller than embalming others' works, dusting off new thrones for the new successors in the public eye. So what remains? I don't know. I know I want to create something, and it's going to have to be different than what is. I don't want to imitate anyone in the world. I want to say something in a way nobody has ever said it before. I suppose dissatisfaction with the status quo makes for progress.

Overleaf, left:
A yeoman on the
T. B. Robertson

Overleaf, right:
Officer reading

July 25—Off the coast of Normandy

This morning I saw the greatest manifestation of our airpower in all my months overseas, and in particular here in Normandy. For 2 hours we watched wave after wave of bombers move across the sky and head for the lines and Germany. It is one thing to read of thousands of planes attacking, and quite another to see it. It was incredible. No sooner would one wave pass over our heads than another would appear as tiny specks in the distance and with a grace of movement impossible to describe, they would arc across the whole roof of the heavens. Then, humming quietly, they would move away to be replaced by still another and another and another wave. It staggered the imagination, and I couldn't help but imagine the reaction of the German lads in the lines as they watched these multitudes of aircraft wheel over them. Our power grows steadily. When it explodes in all its force, the results will be irresistible. The Russians are starting on the stretch, and every front is moving closer to the festering point of this whole horrible infection. I hope to God that this time there is a finality to it all. We will never be this lucky again.

I WAS REMINDED by the following letter of how often we worked as our own censor when writing home during the hostilities. Why burden your wife with gratuitous horrors or descriptions of frightening events that could only contribute to her anxiety and apprehension? Instead you alluded to "something that took place here," a banal marker which could remind you for sharing once you were together again at home.

Sometime in July—Off the coast of Normandy

I worked on and off all day on a detailed sketch which will be part of an illustration I'm going to make. It's of something that took place here shortly after D-Day, and it's been on my mind ever since. It's not at all the kind of work I'll probably ever do again, but I want to get the whole thing out of my system.

THE ENGLISH CHANNEL is always a restless and moody body of water. In the long months of preparing for D-Day in our tiny craft, we had learned to mistrust the capriciousness of the Channel's weather. In a twinkling, a sunny and bracing day at sea could be transformed into an angry, dark, and wind-driven maelstrom of waves and spray that could swamp our open boats and scatter the whole flotilla of invasion craft. Had D-Day not been postponed a day, the Channel's fury could have aborted our landings and drowned any hopes of achieving surprise or success for the invasion. Eisenhower's decision to wait the extra day permitted us to dodge the bullet and secure the Normandy beachhead.

Shortly after the invasion, on June 10, we had lived through the horror of such a Channel storm. For three days and nights the savagery of that storm nearly destroyed our entire beachhead. All that protected our fragile toehold in Normandy from the full wrath of the sea was our "gooseberry"—old merchant ships and freighters that had been towed across the Channel to act as our only seawall. When the bottoms had been blown out, the ships settled on the bottom of the Channel, their superstructures jutting from the water like so many sandcastles on a holiday beach. When the worst storm in decades began to lash the invasion beaches, our ancient sunken ships

Overleaf:
The gooseberry at
Utah Beach

became our only protection from the wind-driven rains that swept in from the North Sea.

Outside the gooseberry, the waves began to pile higher and higher, crashing against the old ships in a mounting crescendo. The wind was howling through the rigging, and sheets of spray were flung as high as the masts. Inside the gooseberry, a struggle began to secure the hundreds of barges and small boats that were thrashing in the waves. With the other small-boat officers, I was trying to tie down our LCVPs by securing them inboard of the sunken freighters. By midday we had done what could be done and clambered aboard the gooseberry to ride out the storm. It was then that we sighted the LST that was making its laborious way toward our beachhead. In the hollows between the cresting waves, the great bow doors of the ship would be almost lost to view, then rise again, water cascading across her decks. As the LST approached the gooseberry, she swung wide to port, hoping to make a run for the beach. It was then my boatswain spotted the hundreds of army troops on deck. They were in a long, ragged line stretching the length of the ship, waiting for chow. Now they were stumbling and falling on the heaving deck as torrents of water threatened to pitch them into the sea.

"Jesus Christ! A chow line in this shit?" The boatswain handed me the binoculars just as we felt, and then heard, an enormous explosion. As I wiped the water from my glass, I

This page and overleaf:
Disaster in the Channel

suddenly could see the nightmare that was happening two hundred yards away.

The LST had hit a magnetic mine and simply been eviscerated. The center of the ship had been blown away, and the crashing seas were racing between the remains of the bow and the stern of the sinking ship. Her small boats had been blown from their davits and dangled from the wreckage on their useless lift lines. Some dazed men still clung to the wreck, but most had been hurled into the furious Channel. Their screams and shouts were almost lost in the rising wind as we all raced to our boats to attempt a rescue.

As we cleared the gooseberry, the full power of the storm caught our open boats. Our bows would be hurled up on a wave and then come crashing down, filling our small deck and making our footing treacherous. Trying to reach over the gunnels to grab the desperate hands was nearly impossible in the churning water. On every side frightened and bloody faces would simply slide from sight.

"Where are the fucking lifelines?" I screamed. "Not a fucking line on this goddam boat?" All of the invasion small boats were supposed to have installed them for emergencies like this, and the boats in my personal command

had done so in the weeks of preparation for D-Day. In our race to the rescue boats, we had all simply jumped into the nearest LCVP and headed out to the wreck. And on this boat someone had "goofed off," been lazy; and now I was watching kids die who should have been saved. It was a bad dream, and it was happening in maddening slow motion. Fewer and fewer voices could be heard over the wind, and we searched desperately for bodies still afloat.

In a momentary lull, we were able to pull one wounded GI into our boat. A deep gash cut across his drenched uniform, and blood was oozing from his open abdomen. For the first time I tore open one of the packets of sulfa and treated the wound. "We've got to get him out to one of the command ships," I told the coxswain. We covered the shuddering soldier with our soaked jackets and finally delivered him, barely conscious, to the medical help he needed.

By the time we returned to the site of the explosion, all signs of life from the sunken ship had disappeared. Only the tip of the bow was still silhouetted against the lowering skies. All I could think of was the son of a bitch who hadn't done his job. Depressed, drenched, and chilled to the bone, we came alongside a ship riding at anchor inside the gooseberry. "You guys hungry?" I asked. "Hell, yes!" was the response. Even horror couldn't stop the appetites of twenty-year-old sailors, nor mine. We clambered up the ship's ladder in time for supper. But the face of our wounded soldier, so frightened, so pale, kept intruding. I saw his dog tag again, dulled pewter, dangling against his open wound. Kid from New York. Name was Farley. I wonder if he made it.

August 17—T. B. Robertson

Young men dying seems to me, somehow, the greatest tragedy. The acceptance of death has been something new to me. And I know that death serves only to accentuate the love of living we both share so dearly. The bridge between is so complete, so final that you finally stop thinking of its terrible proximity and cling rather to pulsating life. Your laughter is a little quicker, your thinking is a little less shallow, your energies and ambitions fired with a new urgency.

Sometime in August

What rotten times these are—unfair, blundering, wasteful. And yet you believe in the ultimate right of our struggle, the fundamental justness of the sacrifices. So you file away your desires and do your job. How ardently I wish to do that job...and end it. I reserve the right to bitch at what it is—and work for, pray for, and believe in what ought and will be.

LIFE ON THE *T. B. Robertson* gradually settled into a routine. Nominally, I was the hydrographic officer of Utah Beach. In addition to mapping the area, it meant keeping charts of the safe anchorages off the beachhead and helping arriving ships to those areas. As more ports became liberated, the urgency of the work eased and time began to lengthen for those of us still on the beachhead. For many it became a formidable burden to bear. For me, I found the

Above: Mike in his boxing shorts

Left: Navy coxswain

Artist at work—with the inevitable group of onlookers

solace of reading and the pleasure of drawing the people who shared my life a buttress against the depressing sameness of the passing days.

Sometime in August—T. B. Robertson

Quite a fine day. Had a steak and did a watercolor, and all in one day! Had Mike, one of the stewards, pose for me in his boxing trunks. I had a wonderful time with the sketch. I've been using the watercolors now. Some of the sketches have just been spotting colors, drawing with the brush. The color is put on fast and is just suggestive. It's kept wet, and the drawing with the brush imposed on it. They hold a lot of promise. This "sock and leave" method is right in harmony with my temperament these days. No muss, no fuss, no nuthin'. Maybe something will come from all this.

Invariably when I sketch, a bunch of enlisted men gather around to watch. I've been delighted to find things in some of them I either never knew or had forgotten. Many of them are really and honestly interested and excited by drawing and color. Some of them sit near me and don't say a word— just watch. They're just curious to watch pictures being born, but they're always there. It's funny. The tough language falls away, the laughter is quieter—and they're just kids again. I don't really mind at all. The effect of the war on these 17- and 18-year-olds makes them a jangly, discordant, and raucous gang. The veneer is pretty tough, but then you catch a glance, a word, a silence, and you remember it's only a veneer. They're just kids.

LCVP on deck

Crew off duty

August 23—T. B. Robertson

Such wonderful news today! Paris has fallen!

August 24—T. B. Robertson

Big news again today…Marseilles liberated, Rumania kicking in, advance everywhere. We seem to be going like a physic. This whole port direction gang may be moved into some port to keep it going. If that is so, I might be sent right along. If I've got to be working overseas, I'd rather be here than the Pacific. Also, I'd rather be in a port where I can see something besides water and beach and the same old tub day in and day out. You can't imagine how confining that gets to be.

115

August 25—T. B. Robertson

Been a real long day but quite full. The early rising is not too tough to take on the lovelier mornings like this one. The sun comes out of the Channel and floods the sea and the sky with a fresh beauty that would never be believed on canvas. And the day breaks with a dewy delicious rapture that defies war and all the tangled machinations of bedeviled mankind.

It's going to be strange reading over these letters I send you when once again I am with you. They are such awfully poor imitations of a mirror. When I get back and we read over some of my "poor man's sermons" together, I won't have the vaguest notion of what was eating me at the time. These intermezzo epistles are such lousy excuses for living and loving.

August 31—T. B. Robertson

This morning I heard the classic remark of our protracted stay here off Normandy. We had to pass some instructions to one of the newly arrived Liberty ships fresh from New York. One of our sailors leaned far over the rail and yelled up, "Got any souvenirs from the States?" It's really symbolic as hell. The shiniest Kraut belt buckle and the meanest looking Kraut helmet or knife or rifle would now be considered a fair swap for a cold Coke or a glass of Budweiser! The luster of souvenirs has dimmed with every passing day, their value varying inversely with the increased dreamings of home. The noose is sneaking up on Schicklgruber's neck every hour of the day, and the guys are thinking of home. Today it's Czechoslovakia; the Russians in Bucharest. Americans beyond Nice. Things are bubbling.

Opposite:
Cutting spuds for chow

Above: Checking gear
Right: Break time

Sometime in August

One of these fine mornings I'm gonna wake up and find that the U.S. Navy is no longer operating on the beaches. My beach is but a name in a history book. When the ports are enabled to get to work again, my job will be over. So what then? I haven't the vaguest idea. All we can hope for is that we may get home for a while before going elsewhere. I don't think that many of us dare hope for much more. But the war is not over by a damn sight, and the navy is eager to have me stick around. Like seven million other guys, I'm walking through a long, dark cave. Nothing to do but keep walking and praying.

ONE NIGHT, TWO OF THE OTHER ENSIGNS confided that the next evening they were catching a ride to Paris in the back of a truck that carried mail from the beachhead. "Going to Paris for three days," they said. "You want to come?" I said, "Paris? Yes! Hell yes!"

I brought along a bag of sugar doughnuts from the galley to sustain us on our trip to the City of Light. And early the next evening, we three junior officers scrambled aboard the mail truck in a pouring rain. The tarpaulin that stretched back from the cab of the truck was just long enough to shelter the bags of mail. So, in our soaked dress blues, smeared with confectionery sugar, in unrelenting rain, we arrived at a navy hotel—three dead-tired American liberators from Normandy.

After all these years, those next three days are sharply vivid vignettes, unconnected in time sequence but unforgettable! There was the afternoon the three of us found a small bar in Montparnasse. Fernando, the bartender, had fled Franco's Spain and then been trapped in Nazi-occupied France. How we found this out, I cannot imagine, because Fernando spoke no English, and we spoke no French or Spanish. But Fernando liked us and during that long afternoon, as the rain continued to pour down, he taught us the joys of drinking absinthe. Absinthe! In Paris! I thought I had never been happier.

By nightfall, the rains had ceased and we three, much the worse for the absinthe, made our way to the Etoile. Far down the Champs Elysées, we could see the Arc de Triomphe. Arms about each other's shoulders, we set off down the boulevard, singing happily and walking in the very middle of the street. What is most memorable about that long hike is the fact that only one vehicle, an American jeep, passed us! Paris, without petrol, was like a nineteenth-century town. At night in bed, we could hear the clip-clop of horses pulling wagons of vegetables into the heart of the city.

I have never savored walking more than on those three days in Paris. Only half lit from lack of fuel, unwashed and unswept during the bitter years of Nazi occupation, the city still retained her great beauty and magic, at least for me. The boulevards I had imagined from Victor Hugo; a serene but unscrubbed Notre Dame; the graceful series of bridges that laced the two sides of the Seine; cityscapes and parks painted by Pissarro and Manet, whom I had studied at Syracuse; the expatriate cafés I had read about in Fitzgerald and Hemingway; Parisian women still looking elegantly chic in their pre-war dress; and the wonder of the kiosks, bursting with news of Parisian art shows, Parisian music, and Parisian cabaret! After the long, lonely monotony of Utah Beach, I felt I had died and gone to heaven.

On one of the kiosks, I read of a retrospective show of the paintings of Pierre Bonnard at the Palais de Tokyo. I left my companions and finally found my way to the imposing building. If there is a single point in time when I fell forever in love with Paris, it was that afternoon. Alone in the great rooms of the Palais, I was able to explore the work of the great French masters. If only my old professors could see their student now!

As I reluctantly departed the final room, I became aware of shouting and pandemonium in the galleries across the corridor. I stepped inside into a scene that was so startling and quintessentially French that it made me laugh. It was the first post-liberation exhibition of Pablo Picasso, a man I had never heard of and an artist who obviously ignited passions of love and rage in two very vocal camps. Some viewers were so angry at the work or furious with the politics of the painter, that they were peeling paintings from the wall, shouting "Communist pig!" Others were struggling to return them to the walls, screaming "*Pétain merde!*" Gendarmes coolly viewed the near-riot as nothing out of the ordinary.

As for me, I was simply stunned by the movement and noise. I felt totally out of my depth when I looked at the paintings but delighted with the vitality of what I was witnessing. There had been a time here in France, I thought, when Bonnard himself had triggered such noisy controversy. What a wonderful city!

When I had traveled to New York City as an art student, I would go through the Metropolitan Museum of Art as if I were visiting a hushed cathedral. The paintings I viewed seemed at a great remove, dead icons to be observed with reverence. But now, this incredible scene that I was witness to here in Paris! Art wasn't dead! It was alive!

It was important! It was worth feeling passionate about! That afternoon, I knew that my professors had been right. And I knew, too, that I would never be content until I could share this marvelous city with my wife.

But all good things seem to end, even in Paris. Too soon the leave was over, and we returned to our watchful waiting on Utah Beach.

September 11—T. B. Robertson
There seems to be nothing imminent about closing up shop here. Utah Beach has been the most productive beach taken, and the navy hates to relinquish it, I guess. So we keep going on our job and waiting for the war to end.

September 19—T. B. Robertson
Oh, what lucky kids we're going to have, Sugar! Daisies and not much brains, but they'll love living. And they'll have the loveliest mom and the brokest pop in the neighborhood! They'll be swaddled in affection and grow up loving. I want to give you so much happiness, darling, that it'll overflow, and we'll need kids like sponges to soak up the extras!

September 22—T. B. Robertson
Today was just one full year of playing "ossifer" and absolutely nothing of import or significance occurred to mark it in my memory! Movie was very swell entertainment, "Sensations of 1945" with Eleanor Powell. Some wonderful dance sequences. Impatience to get home grows every day—and the States is the closest approximation of Shangri-la imaginable!

It must be difficult, hon, for you to sense the delight we experience here just talking about home. There is almost a greed that every guy feels when he speaks of his wife, his town, his family. America looks so wonderful from here, Junie. This "old world" seems truly to be an old world. We're part of a very new world—a shiny, bubbling, moving, speeding, raucous, chrome, laughing, colorful, young world. Just think of it, Junie—the tastes that are so completely "our own," and that we don't even think about in the States: waffles, corn on the cob, milk shakes and ice cream sodas and sundaes and banana splits! Neon lights that say Pepsi-Cola—or Charlie's Drug Store. Refrigerators where the lettuce comes out crisp with drops of water on the leaves—and cold milk in bottles! I haven't had a glass of milk since Feb. 8th! Elevators that fly straight up faster than you can think. A whole rich world of music and art and sensations. A lavish world that stretches to the last reaches of your most enthusiastic dreams and imaginations! Cities that hum.

My God, I must sound like something out of Sinclair Lewis! I hope that central heating and spotless men's rooms haven't made me into an "intolerant American." I don't think they have. Rather than arrogance, I think I'm just tremendously proud and thankful. Babbitt was a fool—he accepted the material as the only measure, the beginning and end-all of living. He was a fool because he thought of gleaming chromium and super sewage systems as the end. He should have gotten on his knees and thanked his thousand lucky stars—and resolved to make himself worthy. We're the luckiest, wealthiest heirs in the world, darling. God knows why—but we are. If only we could take that daring and drive and childlike confidence that has carved out the nearest thing to heaven on earth in only a hundred and fifty years—and weld it into a spiritual and dynamic force for good, we Americans might make part payment on a heritage so vast, so gracious, so unbelievably generous that you can see it only when you are thousands of miles away.

Scuttlebutt in Hold #1

September 23—T. B. Robertson

It gets cold as the dickens down here in Hold #1, and sleeping is wonderful. Somehow lights never go out in our room till midnight or later. There's always something real important to shoot the breeze about, and sleep, when it comes, is delicious.

October 1—T. B. Robertson

In these months away, there has been a great deal of time for reflection. It's not only in the bull sessions. It's a thousand influences around me—a phrase dropped, a letter from you, a Negro paper in the mess boys' quarters, a book, an article in "Stars and Stripes," the long hours of silence in midwatch. They are so many and so little in themselves. But they're there. There have been days I've felt filled with shallowness and insincerity, hours of self-searching after the bull sessions when I wonder if I truly believe what I've so ardently been mouthing. There have been times of sarcasm and moments of

Overleaf:
Rough water in the Channel

cynicism, and times I've felt absolutely right. Are these guys blind? And there have been times when I wanted desperately to believe, to get swept up in a movement, to pledge heart and soul and sweat to something bigger than myself, and play that horse for the rest of my life. I've been like a piano in a public park. Every day someone has picked out a tune or run the scales or made beautiful music. There have been dissonances and repetitious chords...and beautiful music.

I've developed a great impatience, but it's not with difference of opinion. It's with opinionated people, with overbearing or condescending guys in high position, imperfect men who condemn or classify a group with the arrogant flippancy of turning a switch or dropping an insinuation. I think my impatience has become more vocal and belligerent. I'm no longer reticent about making a scene, and I'll probably go through life embarrassing my wife and getting my generous nose whacked repeatedly. But I would so like to channel this heat, this impatience, this desire to slap down the bad. As somebody once said, "He's got the saddle, the whip, and no horse."

October 21—T. B. Robertson

Hiya, honey! It's a rough, windy night, and it's been a likewise day. So likewise that I couldn't get a small boat to a ship 600 yards away where my brother is! Yup, Marv is aboard a ship here—and will be here until the weather slows down enough to unload. He blinked over to this ship today: "Lt. Sugarman wants Ensign Sugarman over for a drink!" I just about busted out of my breeches!

HAD BEEN NAPPING, riding out the foul weather that had stopped all our work off the *Robertson*, when Mike, the stewards' mate, excitedly came in my room and shook my shoulder. "Mr. Sweetenin'! Wake up! There's a Lieutenant Sugarman looking for an Ensign Sugarman. Is you he?" I stared at the grinning sailor and bolted out of bed and raced up to Operations. The signalman pointed to the LST lying off our bow. "Signal came from there, sir."

I stared across the water at the ship, rolling wildly in the windy chop of the Channel. Marvin here? It was too impossible to believe. But how marvelous if it were so! My older brother had been my role model in so many ways, and I had been best man at his wedding. But I hadn't seen him now in over a year. When I was getting my commission at Notre Dame, Marvin was earning his bars as a lieutenant in the U.S. Army at the officers candidate school in Michigan. When June and I married in September, Marv and his wife, Roni, were stationed in Alabama. My kid brother, Bob, served handsomely as best man at my wedding—just before he went off to Cornell in the U.S. Naval Reserve. In my last letter from the folks, they were rejoicing that Roni was expecting a baby, their first grandchild. But not a word that Marvin might be shipping out to Europe. And now, a few hundred yards away, he was coming to Utah Beach! I could just imagine the folks' faces when they got the news!

October 21—T. B. Robertson

The weather got more and more wild, and there was no way of getting there. So tonight I called their ship by radio and summoned Marv to the radio! Although strictly against regulation, it was too great a temptation. And honey, he sounded so wonderful! The magic of a familiar voice from home is something so good it can't be

Opposite:
Brothers' reunion,
Utah Beach

described. Imagine, angel, having Marv right here on my beach! I'm praying I'll get to see him tomorrow, but I instructed him if he gets unloaded before I get there to leave a message at the navy HQ on the beach where he's going. The conversation was pretty crazy, both of us were so damn excited.

"Hey, I understand you're gonna be a father! Over."
"You're telling me! Over."
"I didn't think you had it in you! Over."
"Are you kidding? Over."
"I think it's wonderful! You got a bottle of Scotch? Over."
"Lots of it. Get the hell over here! Over."

THE NEXT MORNING DAWNED bright and clear, and I searched the seas in vain for Marvin's ship. Operations told me it had landed at 0400. I lowered a small boat, commandeered a jeep on the beach, and learned from HQ that Marv's outfit was heading for Cherbourg. I floored the gas and headed up the Cotentin Peninsula. I was overwhelmed at the roll of the dice that had, in a global war, sent my brother through my beach among all the beachheads in Europe and the Pacific.

October 22—Utah Beach

I'm shacking up on Utah Beach tonight. I've just returned from Cherbourg where I spent the day with Marv! Oh, baby! What a terrific thrill! He looked so good—sounded so damn good! We shmoozed and bulled until suppertime. He had a meeting tonight and one tomorrow morning, so I left. But we hope to meet in Barfleur for dinner tomorrow.

*The Hotel Moderne, scene of a
memorable dinner*

A SAILOR WHO WAS PART OF THE MERCHANT MARINE crew on the
port direction ship was the only one I knew who knew the
area. He used to make port in Cherbourg before the war.
"Where can I take my brother for dinner, Billy?" I asked.

"If you're looking for a great meal, go up the coast to the Hotel
Moderne. A little place in Barfleur, right on the ocean. Was great in
'38, but that was before the occupation. It's worth a shot."

Marv's outfit was quartered in nearby St.-Mère Eglise, a short
run in my jeep from the beachhead. I picked him up and we drove

carefully through the still-rubbled streets of the town, then on to the coastal highway that ran up the peninsula to Barfleur and Cherbourg. We found the modest and miniature hotel easily and paused at the entrance. On the walls were rusting medallions, dreaming of happier times: GRAND PRIX 1931, GRAND PRIX 1935, GRAND PRIX 1937. As we entered the tiny dining room, the elderly owner greeted us with "*Bienvenue!*" and led us to a table. I thanked him, and told him that we were about to celebrate a very special occasion.

"I have been on Utah Beach since D-Day," I said. "And yesterday my brother arrived with his army outfit—on my beach!"

The old man's eyes opened wide. "Mon Dieu! Brothers? How marvelous! This is a very special occasion indeed!"

He paused a moment, and then asked us to follow him. He led us through the fragrant kitchen, pausing only to introduce us to the chef. "Tonight we are serving both the American navy and the American army, Jacques. En garde!"

We followed the elderly gentleman out into the small vegetable garden, where he picked up a shovel that leaned against the potting shed. Walking carefully between the rows of beans and carrots, he paused at a flat rock and nudged it aside with his toe. He began to dig, his face concentrated on his labors. He stopped suddenly, and reached into the dark soil. Smiling broadly, he handed each of us a bottle of Muscadet, the moist dirt still clinging to the dark green glass.

"For five years—five very long years," he said, "these wines have hidden from the Boches. Tonight they will celebrate this memorable American reunion!"

"Memorable" doesn't even begin to cover that remarkable evening with my brother and our new French friend.

AT LONG LAST, orders came spelling the beginning of the end of operations in this sector. The *T. B. Robertson* fired up her engines and hauled up her anchor. Now that the ports had been liberated, this war-torn beachhead could once again be a solitary and silent Normandy beach.

For more than five months the *Robertson* had been the nerve center of Utah Beach, and the only home we had known since D-Day. But I would not be leaving with her now. With a handful of other officers, I moved my seabag and gear to an LCI (landing craft infantry), which came alongside. We had been ordered to remain as the last guardians of Utah Beach until final orders arrived, securing the area. It was an odd and autumnal feeling watching the old Liberty ship slowly swing her bow toward England. A fog began to roll across the Channel, and soon the rusting stern of the ship was lost in the gray soup.

The LCI was a slender and cramped vessel, and seemed to roll incessantly even when the Channel was seemingly calm. Cussing our fate, we picked up our gear and reluctantly hauled it below. England, for us, would have to wait a little bit longer. Snafu—Situation Normal, All Fouled Up.

November 2—Aboard the LCI
Well, Pooch, duty on the LCI has begun—and in some respects it looks damn desirable. First and foremost, the executive officer dabbles in oils! And tonight I did the first oil since leaving Fine Arts

The first oil painting

Bunking down

Opposite:
Self-portrait for June

at Syracuse, eighteen months ago! It was a two-hour portrait of one of the guys in the crew. And it felt so good again! Lord, how lucky it is that we can forget how good things we've known really are. Honey, it was like going home…<u>almost</u>!

November 4—The LCI

I feel so strange tonight. I don't exactly know why. You remember that shell of "unfeeling" I used to write you of? That dispassionate mask that locks you (the you that used to be important to your wife, your work, the people that loved you, yourself…) locks you far down beneath the darkness, the cold. And nothing can touch it. How jealously you guard the identity, and you put your own sentries around it—casual laughter, sarcastic banter, the unsubtle, the obvious, the baser self. And down in the darkness, the you that matters slumbers in hibernation. It stirs only when a foreign shaft of light creeps into its darkness, and the quick rememberings are happy pain that lingers on until the last sweet drop of light has been drained and the darkness is complete again. How casual and brittle and flippant I feel, Junie. It worries me. Do people become emotionally sterile from abstinence from warmth and the pulsating reality of living? Of sensation? Of feeling? And yet the living stopped for me nine months ago. It's been like a kid jumping into the lake and trying to see how long he can hold his breath underwater. No, I'm not drowning. But I'm getting goddamn tired of holding my breath. Gee, darling, how glittering and bright it will all be when I bound back up to the surface! I hope for our sakes, sweetheart, that I'll be the guy you once loved.

Life here is easier than aboard the Liberty ship, but in one way, it's damn disturbing. The radio is on continually, and your nice cozy unthinking ivory tower is riddled by wonderful old sentimental songs. So help me, the air raids and strafings and bombings of D-Day and after never shook me like "I'll Be Around" and "I'll Walk Alone." "It Could Happen to You" makes me practically a neurotic case. Remembering is one of the more tantalizing by-products of spare time.

November 9—The LCI

For 10 months I've been awed by the tremendous enormity of war matériel, the thousands upon thousands of planes and tanks and guns and tons upon tons of explosives and death we were amassing on every road, field, and harbor in England and since D-Day have been pouring in through this and other beaches in a fantastic flood that staggers your imagination. But all the time you couldn't forget that this, in itself, was only the surgery. Whether the patient would live was what was really important.

I finished an oil self-portrait, and I hope you like it. It's the first oil self-portrait I ever tried, and it's quite a jolt having to look at yourself dispassionately for hours on end. Outside of a stiff neck and a nervous breakdown, though, I'm really feeling fine.

135

November 14—The LCI

Today I received a grand birthday gift from the navy—word that the operations off this beach are done! Through! Ended! Kaput! Fini! We'll just have to wait a day or two for the last few ships to sail away, and then we go back to England! So anxious to get moving again! You can't imagine how personal an enmity each one of us "survivors" feels for this bastard beach! It's been like being chained to a fire hydrant for five months.

It's such a crisp, lovely night tonight. Walked about the deck and breathed it all in. And like some tantalizing magic, we were shuffling through dead leaves on campus to the "Greeks"...to Suss's apartment...What a beautiful part of living we've already sewn into our time, Junie. Such little things, and so precious—whiffs, touches, breaths of things, glimpses, glances, fragments. Is life like that, Junie? Maybe man knows happiness through a thousand disconnected bits, not by saying, "I will lead a happy life and start here and end there."

November 18—En route to England

At last we're leaving France! It's hard to describe the pleasure I felt this afternoon when I saw white water bubbling behind in our wake, and the beach that had been our neighborhood for almost half a year flatten and fall into the sea. And with it went a whole part of my life. It was a peculiar feeling. On that ridiculous bit of surf and sand and dune, I had seen men die. I had known danger and watched the machinery of war roll through and over us, leaving only the lethargy and boredom that seems to be the backwash of war. As I left, I said a mental thanks—one more dead beach behind

me. I'm feeling fine and in perfect health. What lies before me now I don't know.

November 20—En route to England

I've been playing with an idea for five weeks now. What I'd love to do is work in New York about two years and then take you with me to Paris for six months, maybe a year even. That place has excited me, Junie. Damn but it has. I hardly had a look in four days, and yet somehow I knew. How I'd love to discover it with you. No Cook's Tour, but just coming over and living in it, soaking it up. What fun we could have. To be in Paris with you, when we're still so young. Can you see it? Maybe I'm nuts, maybe the months here in Normandy have truly made a screwball out of me. But I've become so terribly jealous of "living." I've seen enough to make me believe that method and staid order can never be an acceptable dictator to my life. I feel such a crazy impatience, Snoon. I've seen so much I've wanted to share with you, to have you see and love and enjoy. Not when we're fifty or sixty, but when we're still a little mad and very young. The world doesn't seem a tremendous place to me anymore. It's been a funny kind of metamorphosis.

It all seems to break down to this: the only real, the only living part that has been in these places has been me. When first I arrived in Scotland, I pinched myself and said, "Sug, you're not really in Scotland." Scotland was something remote and unattainable, that pink portion of the map, way over there. Those same astounding realizations came when I saw Piccadilly and Berkeley Square in London, on the Champs-Elysées and in Montmartre in Paris. "Not me. Not really. Not here." What I mean is that everything in the world only lives when it lives in you. You don't ever lose anything lovely or strange or beautiful if it touches you. I want what I've seen and touched and experienced to be part of us. How wonderful it would be if we could live in lots of places, live and love and expose ourselves to the strangeness and wonder of "difference" while we're young and curious and adaptable. We have a long, wonderful ways to go together, darling, and I hope that we can take some side roads away from the billboards and drive-ins. The view can be breathtaking.

RETURN TO
ENGLAND

THOUGHTS OF HOME

T HE RELIEF WE ALL FELT at being released from the death hold of the Normandy beachhead was quickly replaced by anxiety and confusion on our return to England. The navy base was alive with scuttlebutt about our next assignments.

"Small-boat officers and crews are going to Germany for the Rhine River assault."

"No!"

"The guys from Normandy are going home to prepare for the Japanese invasion."

"No!"

"We're being sent to Antwerp…to Cherbourg…to Le Havre to man the newly liberated ports."

"No!"

"We're heading home. Heard it from a yeoman at headquarters."

"No!"

By the time I received my orders assigning me to another LST in the European Theater of Operations, I had passed the last promising rumors to June. "Heard that we may be coming home real soon!" I was heartsick with disappointment and guilty as hell that I had raised Junie's expectations.

December 1—England

Received my orders for the LST 357 this morning. So now the foul deed is all wound up. Oh, well, c'est la guerre. Written into the orders is a five-day leave and "proceed" orders, which gives me four extra days, nine days in all. They must have had a bad conscience, the bastards! Think I'll go up to Edinburgh in Scotland. It's supposed to be very lovely, and I never did get to see more than a glimpse of Scotland after we landed last February. Had a marvelous Thanksgiving dinner yesterday of turkey, stuffing, and the "woiks." In fact, physically speaking, your guy is in great shape. Mentally, he could use a physic. Maybe the leave will do the trick.

December 10—England

The leave in Scotland was swell. And for the first time since I've been in the navy, I'm returning for duty really rested up. Got a train after lunch and arrived in London about six. Went to a Red Cross club and made arrangements for a room. Then went wandering through dimmed-out London—and that is an amazing experience, Snoon. Packed and jammed like Broadway and dark as a Scotchman's pocket. You hit Piccadilly Circus and the place is teeming with "Piccadilly Commandos"—"Four pounds, honey…four pounds…" Old bums hawking condoms, and men, men, men. Kids looking wide-eyed, smirking, looking young and tough in their sailor pants and paratroop boots and crumpled up pilots' hats. Wings and ribbons and laughter and cheapness. I wound up in the sudden quiet of a hotel lounge and had a couple of beers. The "commandos" were there, too. But they were with officers, and the laughter was a little more subdued. In the soft light, too much color didn't look so bad.

I kept wandering, catching the half sentences, the giggles, the earnest eager whispers, the strange shapes glued suddenly in the glare of a car's light. The shuffle, shuffle, shuffle of boots and shoes and sandals and pumps on the cement. I'd push into a pub, have a beer, and move on. The funny half world of being high was all mine.

Got back to the Red Cross about one and left a call for early, and by that afternoon I was in Edinburgh. From then on it was one long Cook's tour: St. Giles' Cathedral, the two great castles in town, the art school where I ate in the cafeteria and browsed for hours (what sweet nostalgia!), the Firth Bridge, the shops where I bought you the most beautiful cashmere scarves, the generous and friendly people I met everywhere, the tremendous number of bookshops, which I loafed through at leisure, and the wonderful toot I wound up on last night, knocking off the rest of the chaplain's bourbon. (I'd saved it for something special!)

December 14—England

Today was one of those timeless, blustery, gray fall days when long thoughts reach way out, and you're aware of how alone you are. Maybe you shiver a little bit, but the chill is inside of you. The great transparent arc of gray sky stretches forever, and the curl and endless roll of breakers sweeps in a great fan way out at the end of the quay. Grays and dirty greens, and the feathery whiteness of the breakers. And the endless surge and roll, surge and roll. Eternity must be gray.

Honey, I don't know if I wrote you about this. But just before I went on leave I received a letter from my old LST, the 491. I was terribly shocked to hear that my old bunkmate, Danny Buttabaugh (Badger) was killed. Don't know the details, but apparently it was after the southern invasion. He was killed in a plane crash "flying to pick up mail for the 491." He was an awfully sweet and quiet boy. It's a hell of a break. He was all set to get married, I remember, and used to write his girl when I'd write you.

December 15—England

Fully expect to see my new ship tomorrow, and a little excited at the prospect. What my job will be I don't know, and new duty always seems "very potential." You will probably get groups 'n' groups of letters full of virginal enthusiasm, and then wait for reality to set in. Saw the roster of officers aboard. Skipper is two stripes and everyone else a stripe and a half. I'll be the only en-swine aboard, I guess, at least for another couple of weeks. Expect my promotion will probably roll around somewhere around the first of January. Really makes little difference to me. I've gotten kind of attached to this old lonesome stripe!

December 17—LST 357

I'm writing you the very first letter from my new home, the LST 357. Now for some first impressions. The officers are all young, but I'm the youngest. The skipper, Reynolds, is gray at the temples, has a

Small-boat officer

thinnish face, rather severe eyes. But he smiles a lot, and the old "God is with us gentlemen, let us rise" air that followed in the steps of my last skipper isn't here. This fellow's voice is quiet. At times he seems older than 34. When he smiles, he seems younger. Blackburn, the exec, is a big, burly, vivacious guy. He spars with the enlisted men, cusses the skipper, enjoys himself, jokes incessantly, and seems to know what he's doing. He's about 27, likable as hell. Then there's a big good-lookin' kid named Taylor who looks like a football-playing Deke. He is! There's McElroy. Pleasant enough. Can't figure him out. Either he's awfully sharp or awfully dull. There's Art English, an old small-boat officer, very friendly. As a bunch they seem swell, and I hope the opinion sticks.

December 21—LST 357

Tonight the first Christmas carols came over the BBC, and with it morale aboard ship must have dropped about 80% I guess. Christmas is too tightly wound with "home" for these kids to dismiss it with their usual easy flippancy. The carols sound sweeter and sadder somehow than I ever remembered them. I kind of hope we'll be in England for Christmas. I'm wondering what's cooking for your holidays, darling. I hope so hard that they will be pleasant. I'll be with you in spirit, angel puss. And I think maybe you know that.

December 24—LST 357, under way

The hook just came up and we're off for La Belle France. Santa Claus will have to reach us by a small boat I guess, 'cuz at midnight we'll be cutting our way across the Channel. My first trip over on the 357 was a beauty. The Channel was as slick and shiny as the seat of my blue serge suit, and the weather as docile as could be desired. I stood the eight-to-midnight watch while under way, and it was a glorious experience. The half moon was bright as a new half dollar, and she slipped like some ivory untouchable from one veil of cloud to another. The radio came on and the Christmas carols floated out to the silence, and the mast seemed a great dark cross that rolled against the gray crystal of the wake.

My, my, sugar. How I do go on. But it was beautiful.

Let me tell you what I did yesterday. Went ashore and went to the officers' club. Had a beer and continued my remote appraisal of English women. It's an appraisal which has been going on passively all these months over here without extensive laboratory work. I have decided definite things about them.

1. They are a race apart from the English men. Not only a sex apart, but a race.

2. They seem much nicer than their male counterparts. For the great mass of young American manhood, this preference springs obviously from a certain wantonness and lack of restraint sexually that they surprisingly (to an American bred on "English reserve") display. Whether they have always been thus is a matter of conjecture. Whether because of five terrible years of war, loneliness, the fact that Englishmen are just lousy lovers, or the fuel shortage, I am most inadequately capable of saying.

It's this sexual casualness that appeals to the great mass of the Yanks here. For myself, not being in the market, my preference has sprung from more casual but elementary sources. I've talked with them on trains, at teas, at dances, at bars, in restaurants. They seem to have all the good qualities of the British—a lot of guts. (You meet women 18, 19, 20 who have been on anti-aircraft batteries for years and casually talk about the action they've seen, the bombs that have missed them, the planes they shot down, their losses of brothers and sweethearts and husbands.) They have a good sense of humor, a certain feeling for character and strength that you can't help but sense when you speak with them. Unlike their men, their reserve is not even skin-deep. Their admiration of things not English more ready and less grudgingly given, their admission of English faults more honest, and their intelligence closer to the surface than their brothers'.

There is so much promiscuity that you tend to class it as a group trait, which of course is unfair. Most of them, particularly in the service, are nice, sweet kids. They would no sooner think of sleeping with some Yank than most of our kids back home would. I'm certain they seek the questionable pleasures of necking and petting like our own. When they doll up, they look pretty good, pretty neat. But they don't have the flair for clothes that our gals do.

This discourse is definitely questionable in value, but I thought maybe you'd like my "sum total" reactions.

DUTY ON THE LST was often strenuous and repetitious. Our job was to ferry men and war matériel from England to France, then repeat the process in reverse. We were constantly getting the troops and the cargo squared away for the often rough crossing to the French ports; unloading the overcrowded tank deck in a bedlam of sound and clouds of exhaust; unbolting and unchaining all the packed vehicles on the top deck, moving them to the hold, and easing them out to the frantically busy quays. Once the ship was totally vacated, we'd begin the arduous task of loading the men and the machines that were being sent back to England for repair and rehabilitation. It was draining, exhaustive, endless work. And we knew it was necessary. Still, the occasional leave helped.

On one leave, in London, I arrived to find that the Germans were now firing a more deadly rocket into the heart of the city, determined to break the morale of a very stubborn people. Unlike the V-1 rocket, which one could watch approaching and so was more vulnerable to anti-aircraft batteries, the V-2 came unseen. It simply exploded, devastating entire blocks. Although V-2s were more powerful than their predecessors, I believe their psychological impact on the English was less. When you heard a V-1 rocket cut off its motor, it was an excruciating wait until you heard the explosion. There was nothing you could do about the V-2s. So when you heard the explosion, you knew the worst was over, and you were still all right.

One raw and rainy afternoon I went to Albert Hall to hear Dame Myra Hess give her daily piano concert. The warmth of the crowd helped to warm the great barn of a hall, a mighty Victorian relic. High overhead a glass ceiling arced across the vast room. Once Dame Myra began her Beethoven, the crowd grew silently attentive. Suddenly a V-2 rocket landed a few blocks away. The roar shook the hall violently, and every head but Dame Myra's looked apprehensively skyward. As the glass shuddered and wobbled, Dame Myra played on. To my observation, not a single person left the hall. The ceiling remained intact, and to great applause Dame Myra Hess finished her concert.

Army guard

Overleaf:
Army cargo on the 357

G.I.

Casual officer
— very!

Sketches from Kurt K
my first trip on the
Dec. 14

Undated letter

At 2:30 on Saturday we were at Royal Albert Hall (a tremendous, ugly, Madison Square Garden sort of place and cold), for the Beethoven concert. The concert was probably the real highlight of the leave. It was that good. Myra Hess, the soloist, was excellent and the concertos were played with a humor and delicacy that was really something special.

(My review of Dame Myra's performance, in my letter to June, failed to mention the small interruption of a V-2 bomb!)

December 30—LST 357

Am so happy to hear that our library is expanding, hon. I've developed a tremendous fondness for books since being away. That is one of the few legitimate compensations for solitude. I feel like a sponge that was really never damp before. I soak them up as I read them, and it's shocking what they're doing to my sleeping habits! Finished "Lust for Life," Stone's biographical novel of van Gogh yesterday. What an amazing and marvelous man he was. I'm very grateful to Stone for having written it. I might never have known van Gogh, and I would have been the poorer for it.

My ignorance is amazing, Junie. No kidding. Whether it's our system of education or just me, I don't know. But there is <u>so much</u> I know little or nothing about. History, economics, <u>painting</u>. Christ almighty, I'm almost nakedly ignorant of my own profession. I'm terribly serious. There is so much I should know. I'm embarrassed that I was never really aware of my lack before. How about it, Mrs. Sug. Want to smarten your ignoramus spouse up? It will take at least a lifetime!

152

We have been working very hard and have been at sea almost constantly. Went ashore last night, hon, and had the most remarkable coincidence happen to me. Was in a hotel bar ordering a beer and I noticed this tall, dark ensign standing next to me. I thought I recognized him and asked him if I knew him. He said he didn't think so. "Where are you from in the States?" I asked him. "Cleveland. And you?" I told him Syracuse and said I had relatives in Cleveland (though I'd never been there). "What are their names?"

"The Kane family," I said.

"Kane? Jimmy Kane?"

"Hell, yes! He's my cousin! Alma's brother."

"He married my sister last week!" Can you beat that, Junie? I could hardly believe it. A total stranger at that! His name is Ed Brummel and he's on another LST here in port. He seemed nice and I hope to see him again. That sort of thing has happened to me so often that I think maybe I'm bewitched or something.

On a late December morning, the 357 slowed its engines as it approached the jetty off Le Havre harbor. We were waiting for the harbormaster's pilot boat to reach us. I helped the French pilot aboard and took him topside to meet with the skipper. Viewed from the sea, the harbor seemed to be a jumbled, flattened wreck. Salvage crews were still straining to clear the sunken vessels, and cranes were at work dragging away whole sections of bombed-out harbor facilities. With the pilot's assistance, we headed for a shingled strip of beach beyond the tangled docks. On this trip we were dropping off army troops, and picking up soldiers heading back to England for R&R, after duty in the Ardennes.

As the LST nudged its way onto the beach, the army was ordered to prepare their vehicles for debarking. The excited soldiers raced to unchain the trucks, jeeps, and halftracks that were secured to the main deck. Down below on the echoing tank deck, motors began to roar, competing in the din with the shouts and laughter of the drivers. After the 357 ground to a halt, the great bow doors were undogged, swung open, and the army replacements started driving down the ramp. Only when the caravan had cleared the ship and headed for the mouth of the Seine did I see the men we were to bring aboard.

Lying propped against a low sand dune, the silent soldiers were nearly indistinguishable from the sand. They appeared rather like a strange frieze. They were the color of dun. Their helmets, faces, and uniforms were one muted hue of gray. Nothing moved. Eyes stared, focused not on this ship that would take them back to England and rest, but on the horrors they had just left behind. Less than a dozen hours ago, they had been transported from the hell of the German counterattacks in the Ardennes. There was no indication that they even recognized where they were, or any assurance that their terrible exhaustion would enable them to stand again. As we crossed the beach to assist them, they silently began to rise. Watching these young old men shuffle toward our ship, I silently wept for them. "This is the face of war," I thought. "This is the madness that war is."

New Year's Eve 1944—LST 357

It's 10:30 in the evening. I have the midwatch, 12—04, in a short while. The rest of the guys have broken out all there is to eat, and it's been a noshing evening of the first water. Here on the table are emptied dishes of ice cream and still virginal fruitcake! But hidden—deep in my locker—is one healthy shot of cognac that's resting for five in the morning. OUR toast, McSweetenin'! This year would have been an impossible situation without you, Junie. Someday maybe we'll laugh at it, but I know that tonight the young Sugs are slipping out of the year with a mutual sigh of relief. What's the inventory? As of December 31, 1944, we share a love that has been tried and found so good and true, a determination that is stronger than ever before, an eagerness that is almost unbounded. Please let me say what's in my heart. Thank you, Junie. I love you more than I did in 1943—and less than I shall in 1945. God bless you.

Sometime in January—LST 357

The ship is going into dry dock for a general overhauling. It will be a pleasant break in the ferry boat service for a while. Ridiculous as it sounds, I guess I'll be going on leave again in about a week. Leaves are the most welcome antidote to this routine living that I know. I have few illusions about any of our indispensability, especially mine. So I welcome every chance to break away. It's not that the ship or the work is distasteful. It's a happy ship. But it's almost totally unimportant to me, completely without significance. I fill a job. I perform it. It's necessary. Someone must do it. That's all. It simply doesn't touch me. When I'm on leave I'm divorced from everything nonessential. I can hear music, talk to people who speak my own language, see pictures, get excited, pleased, and even angry. I owe the navy my energy and my ability. I owe myself the complete effort to retain my values, standards, and measures of satisfaction. Leaves help.

January 2—LST 357

A brand new bouncing baby of a year. Yesterday I climbed into blues and took the liberty boat into town at 4 in the afternoon. I decided not to go to the officers' club which, like most, is a stuffy place, and went "a-pubbin'." I'd drop into a bar, hide behind a beer, and just watch. It was swell fun. Every bar is jammed with our kids and the British as well. There's a hell of a lot of noise, smoke, laughter, shouting—a jangled conglomeration of too many young kids drinking too much, yelling too much, smoking too much. But it's real and it's true. "Truth's beauty and beauty is truth"—and somehow the beauty you find in the service is not in a handsome, dolled-up navy lieutenant kissing a gorgeous Powers model. It's in the kids— laughing, sweating kids. Smooth kids from Jersey and New York; big- boned skinny kids from Minnesota; dark, ruddy kids named Tony and Angelo with arms around their picked-up gals. Raucous and loud, caps pushed back on their heads, lights from the bar picking up the matted curls pushing out over their foreheads. Everywhere you look is a picture. You get filled with them. And somehow it's beautiful, because it's real.

Opposite.
Returning from liberty

While my thoughts were turning homeward, the thoughts of June and her friends were turning toward the return of their men. The women had their own bull sessions, during which they struggled to imagine their new lives with their long-absent husbands. And some of their ideas seemed pretty strange—at least to a lonely sailor.

January 4—LST 357

The "bull sessions" you mentioned have me completely baffled, Junie. What do they mean by "marriage?" For myself, and I think for you as well, it's a pretty simple thing. We loved each other so much we wanted to make it a real, growing, vital part of living. Society frowns on two people living without the blessings of the church or the state so we found it not only convenient but delightful to become "married." That made us "legal" and "legitimate." It meant we could live and love 24 hours a day. (And if the pay isn't good, the work's steady.) No "11 o'clocks" or "12:30s," just "overnights." This seems a very fine thing to me. It means our joys are multiplied, our problems shared. We can proceed with the blessings of family, church, and state into a full-time partnership of love, aspirations, and work.

How can you ever give too much love? If these gals are talking of how often they should give their overrated bodies to their husbands, then it's something I can't or won't even try to discuss. The American girl, it seems to me, through a series of taboos and prohibitions that started at the cradle and flourish in the sorority houses and ladies' powder rooms, evaluate the enticement, desirability, and innate virtue of their bodies ridiculously high. They seem to marry to experiment, and when they find the experiment is fine, make their bodies not the marvelous by-product and handmaiden of giving and sharing, but a holy grail to be sought by their poor guys for the rest of their life. The sex remains, the love disappears, and the gal wields it like a whip until finally her Joe is Second Vice President of Kiwanis, and they have enough money to travel abroad for a "second honeymoon." By this time the guy is wondering what happened to his love and his life, and he'd developed an attachment to twin beds

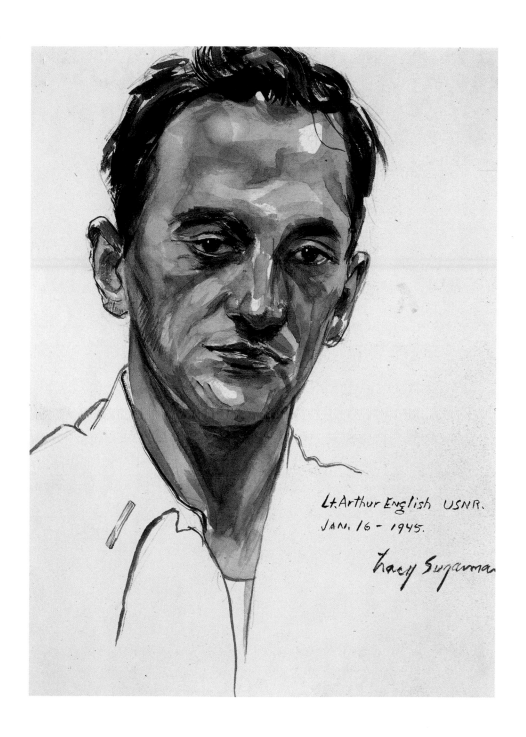

Lt. Arthur English USNR.
JAN. 16 - 1945.

Tracy Sugarman

anyhow. If this is what the gals at home mean, then let them be damn shrewd about it. These guys aren't going home for sex, and they're not going home for locked doors or twin beds. They're going to seek love, companionship, understanding, intimacy, things they can't find in the "Piccadilly Commandos" or the Parisian "Femmes du Soir." I expect that a lot of them wonder what the hell they were thinking about before coming overseas. I don't pretend to know many answers, but this I do know. You're not being "naive" and you're not being "queer." So stop wondering about yourself. Our marriage was, is, and please God, always shall be only an expression of our love. It's nourished by it, grows on it, needs it completely. If it seems "young," then remember we, too, are young. As we grow, it shall grow as well. The girls may do as they please, darling, but love is fragile. They can never woo it with pretense or capture it with reticence. If they give all they have, all they are, all the time, it may touch their lives as it has ours.

January 6—England

Please excuse the V-mail, but I'm dashing it off while waiting for my train up to London. Got a four-day leave yesterday, really a celebration 'cuz yesterday my promotion came through! Yup, my sixteen months as an ensign are now history. It pleases me. Going to boost the allotment, darling, and I'm positive we're now going to be part of the filthy rich! God, if only you were here, what a holiday we could have!

January 10—LST 357, under way to France

Now for the subject of babies, offspring, progeny, etc. etc. etc. Maybe my ideas have changed since coming over here. It's truly hard to

Opposite:
Thatched roof,
Shaftsbury

Overleaf:
Swan Lake Cottage,
home of designer
Cecil Beaton

161

"Swan Lake Cottage"
Shaftsbury England

remember how I felt about a lot of things way back in that "golden age." But as of today, here is how I look at the situation: First, I love you tremendously and so completely that if we never had another person touching our lives, I would feel our marriage was as rich and meaningful. Second, I think children are perfectly peachy. I suspect I always have. I am absolutely awed by the hands, toes, eyes, and tininess of infants. To think we could make one of those perfect bundles absolutely mystifies me. Thirdly, I would like to be the pop of our baby. What's more, I'm certain that it would look just like her mom and be the most gorgeous cherub in captivity. Fourth, I want very much to spend at least some of our really very young years concentrating very selfishly on us. We are both blessed with youth, darling, and even if the war should last two more years, we would be Mr. and Mrs. Doaks at the ripe old age of 25 and 24. There are a thousand things I want to show you and share with you at home and even abroad. Fifth, I am very much of the opinion that when you are absolutely round with child I should be there to laugh at you and help you up the 17 flights of stairs to our garret. Furthermore, I would like to be there when the doctor slaps her *pink little bottom and she cries for her first mink coat. Sixth, I think having a child when we want one would be one of the happiest and proudest moments we would ever have shared. I want it to be something we share, something we want, something we can plan for, something we can anticipate together. If it's that sort of birth, darling, neither you nor I need ever fear that the affection we've known would be diminished one particle. It would be one more of those miracles that our togetherness had produced.*

I am pleased that you like the self-portrait, Snoon. I swear I don't know whether it's good, bad or lousy. Just working again with the oils was so damn exciting that it seemed worthwhile at the time. But as far as the results go, I haven't the vaguest notion. Sending it on to you was a shot in the dark, for there was no one really to appraise the work for me. But if it brought you any pleasure, then it's so much gravy. I used a palette knife a very great deal, though that must be obvious. It's awfully thick—ain't it? ME TOO! Your point of view about your husband's work, by the way, is completely prejudiced—thank God!

February 6—LST 357

It's awful outside—wet, foggy. But here at my desk it's fine. Cuz why? It's really hard to say. Twenty minutes ago my mood matched the weather. But after shaving I suddenly feel wonderful. Someday someone will evaluate the psychological virtues of shaving, and perhaps invent a corresponding "second wind" for our gals. My sudden disconsolate blue mood this morn is just one of those unexplainable spasms that affect lonely lovers, I guess. And the amazing rejuvenation by the homely act of shaving is equally

Opposite:
Painting fog

Overleaf:
Return to port in England

164

unexplainable. This worries me some. For instance, I can see myself, snug as a bug in the rug, tucked into bed with my wife when suddenly I realize I am disconsolate. "Excuse me a minute, darling." With that I throw off the covers, race, nude as a plucked Christmas turkey to the john, and start shaving like mad! Ten minutes later I come back to bed, all smiles, and I find my wife at the window, screaming for help. It's a disturbing picture.

I've been making preparations for the two parties we're giving the crew tomorrow night and Friday, and the men are pretty excited at the prospect. We're getting them a band, a hall, gals, and fifty gallons of beer a night. The last item, at least, should make it a good party! The galley is making sandwiches, cake, and fudge, which I know will tickle the English girls. White bread and chocolate are almost nonexistent in England and have been for almost five years. As a matter of fact, their entire food setup is terribly hard. The only reason I eat well on leaves is because I go to the more expensive restaurants that most civilians can't afford to patronize. There is a ceiling of five shillings ($1.00) on all meals here, but the better restaurants take on extra shillings for "service," "orchestra," etc., and consequently they serve a more expensive dinner without breaking the law. But at the best of the best, you never get more than 1 pat of butter. For the Yanks, the food situation is merely a minor annoyance when on leave, for aboard ship you eat as well as you would at home, often better. But for the English, it's been a long, weary, wearing-down process. After five years of war, they're terribly tired. Dr. Strulli told me almost all of them are suffering from anemia, caused by their complete lack of citrus fruit, very little sunshine, and general short rations. The result is a breaking down of resistance and

Opposite:
Tower of Coombe House,
Shaftsbury

Overleaf:
English Home Guard,
spotting planes

a quicker feeling of weariness. You never hear a complaint. They're the most self-possessed, uncomplaining people in the world. I think it's their great strength, and their great weakness. Endurance and acceptance is a splendid spartan quality. In wartime it's been essential. We can thank God that his English children had such stern stuff in them. They may not win the war for us, but they sure as hell kept us from losing it.

February 19—LST 357, English Channel

It's eight in the evening. All day we've been under way, tearing a dirty cotton fog apart and moving silently along the coast. From the conning tower, you can barely make out the bow of the ship, and on either hand the gray-green water moves silently past and melts into the wisps and dreaming banks of fog. You feel absolutely alone. The whole world ceases to exist, and all that is living is you and the phantom gull that falls and glides tirelessly about the ship. Now it's already dark and the men on the conn are straining every nerve to make out the ship ahead, behind, to the side. I shan't be on watch again till four in the morning, and by then we should be back in our home port. Here at my desk I can feel the low throb and hum, and the intermittent melancholy complaint of the foghorn. It's quiet and I'm sleepy, and I'm quite and absolutely alone with you, darling. How real and tangible our love is tonight! Perhaps there is really nothing more—nothing else in the whole world. Tonight there is no reality, nothing but the remoteness. Tonight there is only our one identity. It's here in the room. It's in the rich quiet inside me, the completeness, the absence of desire, of effort, of need. There is just us. Nothing more is alive tonight. Nothing else begs or breathes or irritates. Tonight there is no loneliness, no fear, no craving, no pain at all. There's just the quiet, the sweet joy of acceptance, the perfect pleasure that steals inside the curtain and brushes my cheek, my lips, my hair. Somehow, if I only knew how, those crazy, wonderful ingredients have joined and blended in this tiny room tonight, darling. Perhaps it's the curtain of fog that has erased the world and built this tiny stage. Perhaps only the good, the true, the beautiful have been spared to come and grace it. For tonight our love has filled this room, and you've been here.

February 23—LST 357

I just wrote a long letter to the folks, the first one in a long time. I've been reading back what I wrote them, and I'm suddenly thoughtful. It's a hell of a vehement letter, and I'm wondering why I wrote it to the folks at all. It's a red-hot discourse on the failings of the American sailor or soldier. It seemed that once I started on the subject, everything just poured out. It's been a subject of growing annoyance and distaste with me.

The inconsistency between the American fighter and the American sailor or soldier is staggering. I remember so well how inadequate I felt when I tried to tell you how wonderful those guys on the beaches were last June. I wouldn't take back a word of it. I feel now as I did then, but coupled with it goes a feeling of wonder. Wonder as to how such marvelous fighters can be such rotten people. The American GI is a source of shame and embarrassment, Junie, and any American that says differently over here is either deliberately lying or he isn't worth a damn himself. Their conceit, their arrogance, their obscenity and vulgarity in front of <u>anyone</u>

shames the life out of me. If they ever had any conception of what we owe anyone, they've forgotten it completely. They never apologize for our own shortcomings, and get a majestic sort of pleasure in making the English painfully aware of theirs. In every conversation we have the "biggest," the "newest," the "cleanest," the "fastest," the most and the best of the good . . . the least of the bad.

Sex to them is anything that wears skirts that they can buy or persuade. Every adjective is a four-letter word, the same one, over and over and over until you could throw up listening to them. Self-respect and self-control are left on the ship with their dirty linen when they go on liberty. Am I surprised? Well, I shouldn't be, and I suppose I'm not. I've seen every one of these things since I've been in the service. But they were spread out and lightened by the rough humor that often accompanied them. But now the rough is coarse, cheap, crude, and repetitive.

Individually, I would do anything for any of them. But as a group they are the antithesis of anything I desire. I don't want to close our eyes and pretend the bad and the wrong and the ignorant aren't there, darling. Those things are real, and too important to both of us. I want only to reject their standards and their values. They revolt and shock me.

Stern and I were censoring the mail when Stern started cutting a paragraph out of one of the letters. He handed it over to me and said, "Take a look at this." It was a copy of that goddamn paragraph that was circulated in the States about two years back. That charming collection of:

"First man to sink an enemy battleship—Colin Kelly."

"First man to set foot on enemy territory—Robert O'Hara."

"First woman to lose five sons—Mrs. Sullivan."

Etc.

"First son of a bitch to get four new tires—Nathan Goldstein."

I was so mad I could have spit nails. I picked up the paper, walked up to the kid who was sending it out and said, "I cut this out of your letter. I don't think it's funny. My brother in France doesn't think it's funny, and my cousin in the paratroops who was killed on D-Day doesn't think it's funny."

I was so angry I came back to my room and sat down. I think I was shaking like a guy with palsy!

THERE ARE UNEXPECTED surprises that one finds when unearthing an intimate record from one's youth. The most astonishing to me are those letters from the war that describe my perceptions of many of the men with whom I served. They swing from admiration to revulsion, from pride to anger, from pleasure in their company to embarrassment at their provincialism and lack of sensitivity. And when the careless locker room bigotry about "lazy niggers" or "avaricious Jews" surfaced, it triggered a deep fury in me and I felt compelled to respond. I pulled rank and only later regretted that I lost the cool I should have kept as an officer.

Yet older is not wiser. Now I still feel compelled to confront the same stupid racism and prejudice whenever I find it.

It is hard to remember how young we all were when we went off to war in 1944. Most of the sailors on my ships really were the "kids" I wrote of in my letter to June. Seventeen, eighteen, nineteen years of age. Put to the test of physical courage, they were remarkable, often accomplishing the seemingly impossible, and usually with pride and good humor. When off on liberty or leave in a war-torn England, however, their ignorance and immaturity often displayed itself in ways that were embarrassing to their fellow servicemen and arrogantly hostile to our hosts.

For the most part, these were kids who had never been away from home, who were fearful and tried to cover it with bravado, who had little or no sense of history, and often showed that they resented being there. American education had ill prepared them to understand how uniquely fortunate their own country was due to geography, not because we were born to be "number one in everything." Nor did most of them understand how indebted we were to those who fought alone for so many years, although the shattered homes and churches and towns around them bore dreadful testimony to the high price that the English had paid for all our freedom. For too many of the Americans, this war was not really our war. It was their war, "and if it wasn't for us Yanks, they'd sure as hell lose it." Thankfully, as a nation, we are a long way from the provincialism that was so rampant in many Americans in World War II.

March 10—LST 357

Another glorious day of calm and sun is dawning, and coupled with the marvelous news that we've already crossed the Rhine, we're all feeling young and gay! Things are breaking at a terrific speed, and all of us are crossing our fingers and praying that the end will come swiftly. It's a funny feeling to be able to actually start to visualize this business over here being done. But it most definitely is in sight, and almost within grasp. It leaves you feeling a little breathless. Our work now is practically divorced from hazard, and our leaves are as recurrent as the seven-year itch. I am learning much about England and the English, finding great hitherto unknown satisfactions in observation and speculation, and wondering what the hell I'm really doing for the war effort! Perhaps tomorrow I'll donate some blood or something. Bad conscience can't live long in all this sunshine, so I know there's nothing chronic in my self-debasement. I merely stretch, inquire as to when dinner is served, and listen with both ears to the announcements of gains being made by guys who are fighting and dying. It's quite a strange predicament. Perhaps I should have the good sense merely to count my blessings and leave well enough alone.

March 16—LST 357

(Scribbled these words on watch at 5 this morning. Maybe you'll like them)

AND THE DARKNESS HE CALLED NIGHT
It's been so long.
But the children are laughing on the beaches
And building caves in the charred and shattered boats.
The dead are buried now
And the grief is dry...and quiet.

They've gone home.
The chill that shivered in the sun
Is hardly an echo—
A thing half-remembered—
Half-heard—
Half felt—
Now,
Good morning, God!

March 17—LST 357, under way in the English Channel

You spoke in one of your last letters of the illustrations in the "Saturday Evening Post." Like you, I think most of them are lousy. The total impression of all the illustrations is that they are being turned out like airplane parts, and have about the same amount of individuality. I've decided that if I must illustrate like that, I'm not going to illustrate at all. The idea of drawing and painting as I want to has occurred more and more frequently to me of late. I think that there might be a market for my work without clearing it through the assembly plant of a magazine or art editor's office. If we have enough dough set aside when I get back to the living, perhaps I'll try. Poor darling. I'll have you starving in that garret yet! This idea has sprung from a lot of things. Psychologically, I suppose it comes in part from the desire for complete freedom that each one of us cherishes over here. But there is still another factor, one that has impressed me even more deeply. I've done enough sketching and fragments of work in these months away to reach certain conclusions. For one thing, the stuff I think is lousy and common and ordinary is the stuff that most of these guys think is great. "Almost as good as a photograph!" The stuff that I think is potentially good—the stuff that delights me in the doing—leaves them puzzled, suspicious, and cold. I have no illusions at all about my being another misunderstood and unappreciated van Gogh. I haven't got that much to say, and could never say it near as well anyhow. But being myself and expressing myself seems very important somehow, even if I have very little to say. Just one more exciting dilemma for our own postwar world, darling.

It's a funny thing to realize that only about 2% of the whole U.S. Navy is still in this theater, and I'm part of it. I know that in a thousand ways I should be grateful for the break, and in about 999 of them I sincerely am. But the other one is the part of my heart that says, "For Christ's sake, Sug, get the hell home to Junie if it's only for thirty days." That is my dearest intention. If it meant an invasion of Mars after 30 days with you, I'd volunteer so fast it would make their heads swim. But there is no particle of choice in the whole deal for us, so we remain. The price of loneliness that I'm paying is terribly cheap compared with those wonderful guys in the lines. They're sweating blood and winning the war, and dodging death a hundred times a day. They're eating rations and sleeping in muck, and waking the next morning to do it all over again. I try not to forget that.

March 19—LST 357

A glorious summer day. Finished "Freedom Road." It certainly is a powerful hunk of stuff, isn't it? Howard Fast writes with a great feeling and passion, and it would have to be a much harder guy than I to be left unshaken by it. Undoubtedly there have been oversimplifications in his work, but the message and the heart of the book are urgent and important. Funny thing to think about, but I wonder what would be the result of compulsory reading in high schools of material like this. Have the kids know of the inherent uncivilized capacities in our people, and have them taste the injustice of our social habits and mores before they become calloused with the easy clichés and half-truths that serve to protect the whites at home from their own sense of guilt. So many of our people who ridicule Hitler's ridiculous race theories subscribe without blush or reservation to the same kind of inanity at home. But our kids don't read material like that in our schools. Why? "Do you want your little girl sleeping with a Nigger?" And that is the end of that. That is the answer to everything. Just ask them. When are they going to wake up, Junie? When are they going to stop being animals that walk like men?

OUR WAR IN EUROPE was rapidly winding down. We listened avidly to the BBC as they reported the imminent joining of the Allied forces in the west with the swiftly approaching Russians from the east. The German war machine was being overrun and destroyed. Late in March, the word we had all so long awaited came from naval headquarters. The LST 357 was to prepare for departure from the United Kingdom. Departure! We were to rendezvous with a flotilla of LSTs and proceed, in convoy, to the United States on April 12, 1945. Going home!

On that exhilarating day when we were finally about to raise anchor for the States, unexpected news came on the BBC: President Franklin Roosevelt had died in Warm Springs, Georgia. As officer of the deck, it was my duty to announce the sad news to the ship's company. Everyone was stunned. For our whole adulthood, FDR had been the only President any of us had ever known. Feeling strangely adrift, we went to our ship stations to prepare for our journey to Norfolk, Virginia.

Opposite:
Yeoman

For June—En route home, April 1945

1944–1945
The sky was lemon-pale, far—so largely whole in its yellow.
The waves chipped hard and sharp white sparks on the pale lemon sea
And the hollows were wet bluegreen.

The ships rolled easy—tethered dumbness—facing the breeze
Like great dull brutes—chained, entranced, following the wind in
Quiet gyrations
All east, southeast, south
All west.
Quiet gyrations—rooted deep in the sea's pastures
And their chains wore garlands of rust that sent shots of color
Quivering on the water.

The beaches were white now—naked they seemed—the spars and hulks
Half buried.
Gentle sand.
The communiqués had thundered past on light-shod stallions that bled
As they ran.
Now there was the kind wind—and the buried bones—
And the ships lying dark on the pale sea.

> *The world is so white and wide, you said.*
> *The sea is so wide. And pale.*

The days were born in the pale east and crept across the hours
Toward salmon pink and lavender.
The street was dusk and squares of electric yellow touched the pane,
The ceiling
The closet door
Lay quiet cool on the floor.

     Days are long, you said—nights are long.
     Hours are sixty and days are seven.
     Months are endless— and the sea is wide.
     Every hour in every day in every month is long. And pale.

The days were joy!
The hours were once around the carousel.
Happy colors of time that shone like a kid's rememberings.
You watched the skies grow lush with blue
And the trees dance verdant with the breeze that kissed your cheek.
Days were laughter in golden air.

     What time is this, you asked?
     What sphere untouched—what music never heard before?
     What dream is this we know
     That once, a year ago, we dreamed?

THE TRIP HOME WAS LONG AND TEDIOUS. Each time one of the ships in convoy broke down, all the others paused to await the repairs. We were at sea for twenty-one days. "Just a shade quicker than Columbus," groaned our navigator. When we finally sailed into the crowded waterways of Hampton Roads, Virginia, we thought we had arrived at Mecca after a very long pilgrimage!

Four days after we landed, the unconditional surrender of Germany was signed. Now all our thoughts were focused on how quickly we could get home to our wives and families. The war was not over. But my war was. And I was going home. To June.

EPILOGUE

I T IS A GREAT SADNESS TO ME that this book captures only one half of an intimate conversation that was carried on through World War II, and for fifty-five years more. Most of the funny, wonderful, life-sustaining letters from June that kept me sane and rooted never made the trip back to the States. Instead, they were read and reread, folded and unfolded until tattered, and finally abandoned when the next sea-soiled envelope arrived.

There is one letter though that somehow survived the chaos of war and made it home. It, too, was in that box of old letters. Written in June's distinctive, clear backhand script, it will give some idea of how special she was.

April 19, '44

Still Wed. night

Sweetheart darling,

There's been something on my mind for days now, but I just didn't know how to write and ask you. But "frank" me—here I am again, & to the point—ahem!! Tell me, snooks, when you think about me all these days—what's the picture, huh? Do you think of me as the "Sweet young thing"—coy & feminine & sometimes cute? I'm really not, pooch—honest! And I'm so afraid that you might be forgetting. Anyhow here goes with a few reminders. 'Kay? First of all, I'm dreadfully in love with my husband. Sometimes to a fault, I believe. I'm jealous as all get-out—but also terribly terribly proud! Also, I want to be made love to <u>all the time</u>—remember? Also, I'm positively fascinated by such horrible things as ingrown hairs—ain't it awful? I'm moody lots of the time. My pet hate is privacy <u>from</u> but not <u>with</u> my husband. Also, I am terribly fond of males as compared with the other sex. I'm an awful nagger when I get started on such things as my husband adopting the responsibility of money, being on time, and picking up things which he has dropped. I like to stay up all nite & sleep all day and am seriously considering a way that we might adopt that sort of life. I love to eat lots & drink lots—and be athletic never!! I'm impulsive as all hell—either love or hate life— & all therein. "Patience" is another item in my lacking list, but I am kinda "smart" sometimes. You tell me so, anyhow.

Well, now I feel much better, for at least you're informed even tho prejudiced, you dopey. And in addition to all this, angel, & above all,

I'm always—

your Junie

I N SO MANY WAYS, June's was a harder war to bear. I knew every day if I was in trouble, what I had to cope with, what I had to endure. June could only guess, pray, and imagine what might be happening to her husband. Yet she was determined to keep up her morale and mine. Every letter was filled with the excitement and pleasures she found in her explorations of New York City. "Can't wait to show you, darling! The things we're going to do when you get home! Oh, baby, just hold on tight and come home!" Art galleries, ballet, theater, the flower stalls on Ninth Avenue, the bookshops in Greenwich Village, discovering "this terrific young guy, Leonard Bernstein!" Balanchine, Alicia Markova, Errol Garner—all were lovingly described so I might share her adventure. My drab seascape would be filled with the color she poured from her blue envelopes. Often, with the letters would come books she had found for us to share. The comfort and joy we both found in those books during those frightening days and lonely nights was to be sustained in all our years of marriage.

When I look at the letters from 1944 and 1945, I see them as a brief, finite interval in our life, only eighteen months in a partnership that lasted for more than half a century. Yet how enormous that chasm of war and separation was to fill! Every week, every month stretched maddeningly slow, and those eighteen months of absence felt infinite.

Perhaps the years of war that we shared should be regarded as a prelude. Within those letters are the themes that were to play out in all our years ahead: our desire to build a life together; to teach the value of love to our children; to be curious and daring; to defy constriction from any direction; to savor difference; to explore new ideas

and new places; to be intolerant of bigotry; to delight in nature; to appreciate the peculiar gifts of friendship; to devote ourselves to work that mattered.

What we could only learn later were the deep satisfactions of building our family: bearing our son, Richard, and our daughter, Laurie; delighting in their growth of heart and spirit; watching with pride as they matured into caring and loving adults, and sharing their joys as they married and began their own families.

My ardent wish during World War II—that someday I might make a singular contribution as an artist—was eventually to be granted. Over the past fifty years I have had the chance to witness and record in drawings and paintings some of the extraordinary people and events of my time. From the Mississippi Delta, I was able to bear witness to the nonviolent revolution of the civil rights movement, a coming together of the races which was to redefine America. From the workplaces and picket lines of the Seventh Avenue garment center, I was able to chronicle the last great labor strike in New York City. From the hollows and abandoned coal towns of Appalachia, I was able to capture the Vista Volunteers who were bringing hope to ravaged lives. From a cross-country tour of European journalists and travel agents, I was able to sketch visitors discovering the grandeur of this land. From the bedlam and nightmare of a Riker's Island holding pen, I was able to show my country some of the bankrupt images of prison life. From a tension-filled courthouse, I covered the everyday drama of the trial of the men who murdered Malcolm X. And I painted the space shuttle Columbia as it inched toward its launchpad and its maiden voyage to space. My life has been blessed with joyous and challenging work. I've drawn rehearsals with Bernstein and Ozawa at Tanglewood, and with the remarkable dancers of the Alvin Ailey Dance Theater at Lincoln Center. I've painted the incredible machinery of corporate America, and the hidden, fascinating life of a great medical center. I've sketched inner-city kids and Ivy League kids, community organizers and jazz sessions with Louis Armstrong. I've painted the glorious legacy of countless New England towns, and the sunbaked, marginal lives of new Hispanic American families in the colonias of Texas. What a privilege it has been to leave my own paper trail across such a diverse and challenging society.

The Good Angel that had guided my toss of the coin before D-Day, sent my brother through my beachhead, and brought me safely home to June from the war, stayed steadfast at our side ever after. Most of what we dreamed of during those difficult days, came to be. We did get to Paris, not as young lovers but with our kids. We did explore the worlds of Italy, Ireland, England, France, Switzerland, the United States, Mexico, and the Caribbean—not footloose, but with our kids, and theirs. We did get caught up in causes larger than ourselves: the civil rights movement, the peace movement, the women's movement. We did embrace theater and the ballet, and learned to love gospel, Seeger, Mozart, and Coltrane. We did try to open doors of understanding by creating documentary films. For thirty meaningful years, June was script editor and researcher for our documentary film company, Rediscovery Productions. Together with our dear friends Bill and Ellie Buckley we were able to write and produce provocative films about the unfinished business of America. Now in colleges, libraries, schools, and community centers, those films, too, are part of the "paper trail."

Opposite:
June Sugarman, 1945

On October 5, 1998, June died in my arms from a sudden heart attack. It was the only thing that could have interrupted our loving dialogue. She is missed daily by so many of us. Especially me. But remembered with much love. Much love.

Westport, Connecticut
June 2000

CREDITS